Praise for *The Money Saving Mom®'s Budget*

"Crystal Paine does it all as an entrepreneur, wife, and mom—and that means she knows all about finding room in a home budget! From reducing clutter to finding amazing coupon deals outside the grocery aisle, *The Money Saving Mom's Budget* will help you make dollars and sense of your life again."

—Dave Ramsey, *New York Times* bestselling author and nationally syndicated radio talk show host

"This book is a great solution for anyone who's struggling with the high cost of groceries and is ready to get on a budget!"

—Mary Hunt, founder of Debt-Proof Living and award-winning author of *7 Money Rules for Life*

"For this mama of six, driving a fourteen-year-old vehicle, endeavoring to live frugally and to live generously, this book not only offers fresh inspiration, it offers a practical, creative plan to make your life priorities—the reality of your life. And her last chapter on contentment? Standing ovation!"

—Ann Voskamp, author of the *New York Times* bestseller *One Thousand Gifts*

"Crystal will save you money, sure, but better yet, she will save you time. Smart home economists know there's no point driving around all day to save $2 when those hours could be spent working, relaxing, or nurturing your family. *The Money Saving Mom's Budget* teaches readers to make wise choices so we can devote time and money to what matters most."

—Laura Vanderkam, author of *168 Hours: You Have More Time Than You Think*

"Are you looking for more wiggle room in your budget? As a mom of ten, I spent years learning to spend our dollars wisely. If I'd been armed with Crystal Paine's book a couple of decades ago, I'm quite sure that my learning curve would have included fewer mistakes. *The Money Saving Mom's Budget* offers real hope to real families who want to escape the cycle of overspending and debt. With a guide like Crystal by your side, you can do this!"

—Mary Ostyn, author of *Family Feasts for $75 a Week*

THE MONEY SAVING MOM®'S BUDGET

CRYSTAL PAINE

GALLERY BOOKS

New York   London   Toronto   Sydney   New Delhi

Gallery Books
A Division of Simon & Schuster, Inc.
1230 Avenue of the Americas
New York, NY 10020

First Gallery Books trade paperback edition January 2012

GALLERY BOOKS and colophon are registered trademarks of
Simon & Schuster, Inc.

For information about special discounts for bulk purchases,
please contact Simon & Schuster Special Sales at 1-866-506-1949
or business@simonandschuster.com.

The Simon & Schuster Speakers Bureau can bring authors
to your live event. For more information or to book an event
contact the Simon & Schuster Speakers Bureau at 1-866-248-3049
or visit our website at www.simonspeakers.com.

Designed by Akasha Archer

Manufactured in the United States of America

10 9 8 7 6 5 4 3 2 1

Library of Congress Cataloging-in-Publication Data is available.

Paine, Crystal.
    The money saving mom's budget / Crystal Paine.
        p. cm.
    1. Finance, Personal. 2. Home economics. 3. Consumer education.
4. Thriftiness. I. Title.
HG179.P178 2012
332.024—dc23

                                        2011026278

ISBN 978-1-4516-4620-7
ISBN 978-1-4516-4622-1 (ebook)

This book is dedicated to my wonderful husband, Jesse.

Thank you for encouraging me to jump way outside my comfort zone back in 2003 when I had a crazy idea to start my own business. Three businesses, countless failures, and nine years later, you're still my biggest cheerleader.

Thank you for believing in me yet again. I love you with all my heart.

CONTENTS

MONEY SAVING MOM®'S 7 RULES FOR FINANCIAL SUCCESS

RULE #1: SET BIG GOALS AND BREAK THEM DOWN INTO BITE-SIZED PIECES

Month 1

Action points: Brainstorm three goals and break them down into yearly, monthly, and weekly goals; set up monthly Goal Accountability Meetings.

RULE #2: STREAMLINE YOUR LIFE AND CUT THE CLUTTER

Month 2

Action points: Create a Personal Priorities List, implement a Time Budget, go through your house from top to bottom.

RULE #3: SET UP A REALISTIC, WORKABLE BUDGET

Months 3, 4, and 5

Action point: Take the Three-Month Budget Challenge.

RULE #4: TAKE THE CASH-ONLY CHALLENGE

Months 6, 7, and 8

Action points: Cut up your credit and debit cards (or stick them in the freezer!) and take the Cash-Only Challenge.

RULE #5: USE COUPONS

Months 9 and 10

Action points: Start collecting and organizing coupons, begin menu planning based upon what's on sale at the store and what you have on hand, practice the Buy-Ahead Principle, become an advanced couponer, try your hand at other ways of lowering your grocery bill.

RULE #6: NEVER PAY RETAIL

Month 11

Action points: Look for creative ways to cut costs on items you need or want to purchase; find ways to have fun—on a dime.

RULE #7: CHOOSE CONTENTMENT

Month 12

Action points: Make a Gratitude List; stop comparing yourself to others; become a giver; choose to bloom where you're planted.

INTRODUCTION

Harried, hurried, overworked, overwhelmed, cramped for time, stressed, frustrated . . . Do these words describe you? Do you feel like you're constantly being pulled in a hundred different directions? Do you go to bed at night feeling more tired and behind than you were the night before? Do you wish you could get your finances under control and stop spending more than you make but feel so far behind that brushing your teeth and showering every day feel like accomplishments?

This book is for you. It's not a get-rich-quickly manual. I'm not going to tell you how to make millions off the stock market. Nor is it a volume on bizarre money-saving tactics that require hours of time to reap a few cents in savings. (I promise I won't recommend recycling toilet paper or stuffing your pillows with dryer lint!) Instead, I hope to come alongside you with simple, proven advice to help you get back on your feet and in control of your finances, to start telling your money where to go, and to begin experiencing the peace that comes from financial freedom.

Saving money is going to take time and hard work. If living beneath your means or saving sixty-five percent on your grocery bills were effortless, everyone would be doing it!

However, I'm convinced that anyone committed to changing their financial situation can do so—if they are willing to change their habits, to persevere even when it's tough, and to keep their eyes set on the end goal. The long-term benefits of short-term sacrifices and determination can be incredible.

Maybe you have piles of debt and are always behind on payments. Maybe you feel stuck in a job where you're barely keeping your head above water, and you have two children and a dog to take care of, too. The good news? You're never stuck—unless you *choose* to be. You can choose to set goals, work hard, get creative, persevere, and make wise choices. Ultimately, these wise choices can propel you to greater financial success than you've ever dreamed.

So what are we waiting for? Let's get started!

CHAPTER ONE

IF YOU DON'T KNOW WHERE YOU'RE GOING, ANY TRAIN WILL GET YOU THERE

Our culture is prone to impatience: we have fast-food restaurants, microwave meals, instant coffee, disposable diapers, and overnight shipping. Every day, we are bombarded with information: how to live longer, lose weight, and make more money—within minutes. Everyone is looking for a quick fix—the one-step program to "have it all."

I wish I could tell you that there's a simple two-minute plan you can implement and become a millionaire tomorrow. While you might see advertisements promising you ways to make $1,000 per day with little or no effort, shortcuts and gimmicks to financial freedom will ultimately fail and land you back in the same place you started—or worse. There's no way around it: true financial success is bred and born of patience, sacrifice, hard work, determination, and discipline.

Until you stop messing around and start getting down to

business, you'll likely live your life running around in circles, never getting a handle on your finances. As I've run Money SavingMom.com over the last five years and interacted with thousands of readers in person and through email, one thing always astounds me: only a few people know how to take the first step toward financial stability. Oh yes, many people have lots of great big ideas—they want to make a million dollars or move to a bigger house or land a six-figure salary. However, very few people know how to make their ideas reality. But guess what? You can! It starts with a very simple principle.

RULE #1: SET BIG GOALS AND BREAK THEM DOWN INTO BITE-SIZED PIECES

You have a choice: you can stand and gaze at the mountain you want to climb and think about how it's too steep, too treacherous, and too overwhelming because you have too much debt, too many bills, or too small an income to get to where you want to be. Or you can map out a way to reach the summit, put on your mountain-climbing gear, and take the first step, and the next step, and the next: paying down one bill, saving up for a big purchase instead of buying on credit, or clipping coupons to cut your grocery bill. Even if you don't succeed in climbing all the way to the top (though I hope you do!), if you don't know where you're going and don't take the first step, you'll never get anywhere at all.

A can-do, committed attitude can propel you to greater financial success than you ever dreamed. Don't waste another moment sitting and sulking about your struggles, or how you wish you had more money, more time, or a better job. Commit to change right now. The *only* way to gain traction and make significant progress is by setting specific, realistic, written goals and then breaking those goals down into bite-sized pieces.

HOW TO BEGIN GOAL SETTING

1. **Clear out a one-hour block of time in your schedule this week.** That might not seem possible if you have a jam-packed calendar, but I promise it will be worth it. Skip your evening television ritual, get up an hour earlier, or find some other creative way to squeeze it in.

2. Sit down with a blank piece of paper (or use the chart on page 187) and **ask yourself, "Where do I want to be financially five years from now?"**

3. **Write down everything that comes to mind:** the big ideas, the little ideas, the sane ideas, and the crazy ideas. Write them all down; there are no wrong answers. (Well, if you say you want to amass $50,000 in debt, that's a wrong answer!)

4. After you've brainstormed a bunch of ideas, **go back through them and choose three goals.**

- Pick one financial goal that you are sure is possible in the next six months to a year.
- Pick one financial goal that you think you could reasonably achieve in the next few years, if you really set your mind to it.
- Finally, pick one financial goal that you love but that feels like a near-impossible goal.
- Note: *If you have credit card debt, car loans, medical debt, student loans, or any other consumer debt, paying it off should be your primary goal. Once you've paid off your consumer debt, prioritize paying off your mortgage or saving for a large down payment on a home.*

5. **Write down your three goals.** If you often feel like you are spinning your wheels and getting nowhere financially, this one step will change everything about how you view your money. Writing down your goals focuses your energy and allows you to start moving forward toward a specific target. Your written goals become your financial roadmap, giving you purpose even during the most mundane day-to-day tasks, like grocery shopping. They also serve as encouragement for you to press on, even if you have a month of unexpected bills and setbacks, or if you're going at a slower pace than you'd hoped.

6. **Break your goals into bite-sized, measurable pieces.** Figure out what you need to do over the next five months or five years (depending upon the goal) to accomplish each of your goals. Break these goals down into yearly chunks, break those yearly chunks down into monthly

chunks, and then break the monthly chunks down even further into weekly chunks. If you're struggling to break a goal down into bite-sized pieces, start with *when* you want to accomplish the goal, and work backwards.

For instance, if you want to pay off $1,500 in credit card debt over the next 12 months, divide $1,500 by 12 months. This gives you a figure of $125 per month. Divide the $125 monthly goal by four to get your weekly goal of $32 per week. Determining the weekly amount of $32 gives feet to the goal: now you know exactly how much extra you need to make or save each week in order to pay off that $1,500 credit card in the next year. While $1,500 may seem like a big amount—especially if you're living on a tight budget or struggling to make ends meet—once you break it down into the bite-sized piece of $32 per week, it becomes much more realistic and doable.

It's not enough to just have that dollar figure, though. You also need to have a specific plan for how you'll actually come up with that extra money. Will you work a few extra hours each week? Have a big garage sale or take on an extra side job? Cut or lower some of your expenses? Think through your monthly spending and see if there's something you can reduce or eliminate for at least a year in order to accomplish this goal.

I'll be sharing hundreds of ways to lower your expenses creatively in the following chapters, but for now, if you can't come up with any way to scrape together an additional $32 per week to put toward your $1,500 credit card debt, then you probably need to go back to the drawing board and extend your time frame for completing the goal to something more realistic. Maybe you need eighteen months or twenty-four. The last thing you want to do is set yourself up for failure from the get-go.

Some of your financial goals might not be so concrete. For instance, if you want to increase your income by $500 per month, developing a plan of action isn't going to be as clear-cut. You'll probably need to allow for some variables. But don't let that keep you from setting the goal and breaking it down into bite-sized pieces. You can still come up with specific, measurable things to do on a weekly basis to put you where you hope to be in a year, five years, or ten years from now.

7. **Post your goals in a conspicuous location and review them often.** Every month, track your progress at a Monthly Goal Accountability Meeting and be encouraged by the traction you're getting. This is your opportunity to review your progress from the past month, pinpoint areas you struggled with, consider ways to make faster progress in the future (could you cut another unnecessary expense or further reduce a necessary one?), reassess your goals, and see if they need any tweaking. Even if you end up taking longer to accomplish the goal than you'd hoped, you'll still be much further along than if you never set a goal in the first place. And who knows? Maybe you'll end up reaching it sooner than you'd even thought possible!

8. **Reward yourself for a job well done.** One of the best ways to keep yourself motivated is to reward yourself for

accomplishing goals. Knowing there's a reward at the finish line can give you greater motivation to keep pressing forward. If your timetable for completing a goal is longer than six months, choose specific milestones to celebrate along the way—say, a reward for each time you hit another 25 percent in savings or pay off another 25 percent of that particular credit card.

WHY YOU WON'T GET ANYWHERE WITHOUT SETTING GOALS

Am I really telling you that something as simple and uncomplicated as setting goals will help you pay off your $15,000 student loan or pay cash for a car? Absolutely. Although it sounds straightforward, goal setting is more than tacking a list to your bulletin board: it's a mind-set.

Goals Give You Purpose

I love watching the Olympics every two years. The dedication and determination of Olympic athletes never ceases to amaze and inspire me. Many of these athletes spend the bulk of their lives training, preparing, and practicing for the Olympics. They want to be the best that they can be and, ultimately, take home that much-coveted gold medal.

Do you think they'd have the same kind of drive and determination to keep a grueling workout schedule if they didn't have a goal of participating (and hopefully bringing home a medal) in the Olympics? Likely not. There would be no reason to miss sleep and social events or put in massive hours at the gym if the Olympics (or another big competition) were not at stake.

Goals give meaning to your efforts. Without a goal, you have little motivation for putting forth effort. However, if you set a goal to pay off debt or to save to pay cash for something, there is going to be much more incentive for driving an old car instead of buying a new one or clipping coupons and bargain shopping instead of just buying whatever looks good at the store. When you know your money-saving activities are ultimately going to push you closer to your end goal, you are much more apt to actually stick with them.

How Lindsey Used Goal Setting to Jump-start a Photography Business

My friend Lindsey and her husband have four young children and live on one income. Lindsey loves to take pictures and is hoping to start a photography business. However, she knew that the only way she could refine her photography skills sufficiently to earn a side income was to upgrade from a point-and-shoot camera to an expensive camera.

Now, Lindsey and her husband are very frugal and creative with their resources, but they don't have a lot of wiggle room in their budget for extras—especially things like a pricey camera. Instead of going out and buying the camera on a payment plan, as she was tempted to do, Lindsey decided to pay cash for the camera. On their tight budget, this seemed like an almost impossible goal. But she didn't let that deter her. She figured out how much she needed to save and then began thinking of specific things she could do every week to work toward that goal. She came up with the idea of offering "Fun Fridays"—an opportunity for moms to drop their children off for a few hours on Friday afternoons for games and activities. She also accepted a cleaning job she could do for an hour and a half once a week while her husband watched their children.

She set aside the income she earned from "Fun Fridays" and the weekly cleaning job into her camera savings account. She tracked her savings by percentages and would update her Facebook status every few weeks with how much closer she was to her goal. We all cheered for her as she inched slowly closer to the finish line.

After cleaning 34 toilets, vacuuming and dusting 190 rooms, and babysitting for 25 hours over the course of four months, she reached her savings goal and paid cash for a brand-new camera. She was thrilled—and we were all thrilled for her, too. She told me that waiting to save up to pay for her camera was so hard, but the reward of putting forth all that effort toward a goal was every bit worth it and made her appreciate her camera so much more. Plus, while she saved, it gave her time to research which camera offered the best features for the best price, and she ended up getting a different—and better—camera than she was originally planning to purchase.

I love Lindsey's enthusiasm and can-do attitude. She didn't sit and complain because buying a new camera seemed impossible on their budget. Nor did she go out and buy the camera on credit when she couldn't afford it. She set a big goal, she broke it down into bite-sized pieces by determining what she'd need to do on a weekly basis to reach that goal, and then she got to work. And her patience and persistence paid off because not only does she now have a brand-new, paid-for professional camera to start her photography business with, she has experienced a great sense of fulfillment by working hard and reaching a goal.

When you set a big goal and then have the patience and persistence to stick with it, even when it's hard and monotonous, you will reap amazing rewards.

Goals Give You Accountability

If you don't have written goals, it's easy to spend money like water. There's always a new outfit or piece of jewelry or electronic gadget to buy. If you don't have a plan for your money, you might as well spend it, because you've not set a true purpose for it anyway. Goals keep you on track. It's much easier to pass by that half-price sale at GAP if you know that wearing last year's dress to this year's party is bringing you one step closer to being debt-free.

How We Paid Cash for Our House

My husband and I were both blessed with parents who taught us the value of hard work and financial stewardship from the time we were young. We had both lived at home, worked, and saved as much as we could before we got married. So the money we had saved, coupled with money Jesse received when his mom died, allowed us to have $35,000 in cash and no debt going into our marriage. We earmarked this savings for a specific purpose: three years of law school for Jesse.

We were both committed to continuing to work and staying out of debt while Jesse was in law school. Already thrifty by nature, our self-imposed beans-and-rice law school budget pushed us to take frugality to a whole new level. In the process, we discovered dozens of ways to squeeze a dollar out of a dime, creatively maximize the mileage of our money, and even how to buy all our groceries and household products for only $35 per week. Our scrimping and pinching pennies paid off as Jesse graduated from law school in 2006—without any student loans or debt of any kind.

After law school, our income increased significantly, but we decided to continue to live simply and save up for an audacious goal: paying cash for our first home. Since we didn't have any debt, we had a good income, and we lived in an area where housing prices are lower than in many parts of the country (it is possible to find a starter home for $100,000 to $110,000 in our area), we knew that this goal could be achieved—if we were willing to stay focused and persevere. We'd already experienced the amazing fruits of focused intensity during law school, so we were excited to set an even bigger goal to work toward.

We spent time discussing this goal and determined that we were willing to wait up to five years to buy a home. Because we didn't have any debt and were able to live on quite a bit less than we were making, we calculated that if we continued to live simply and frugally, it would be possible to save for a house within five years. Even while paying rent, this would put us in a better position financially than we would be if we saved up for a down payment, got a fifteen-year mortgage, and paid it off in less than ten years.

Once we had the five-year timeframe in place, we researched and determined the lowest price we could likely buy a decent starter home for. We divided this number by sixty (since there are sixty months in five years), and came up with the amount we needed to save each month in order to buy a home in five years. This specific monthly savings goal made us *accountable* for how we were spending our money. We carefully considered every purchase and, much of the time, found a way to make do with what we already had or go without in order to throw more money toward our house savings goals.

We didn't always hit our savings goal each month that first year. Life happened, cars broke down, and medical expenses came along, but we never lost sight of the goal. We sat down at the end of each month and had a Monthly Goal Accountability meeting to assess where we were and the progress we had made. Seeing the ground we were covering each month and how we were slowly inching toward our goal motivated us to continue driving an older car, packing lunches instead of eating out, shopping at thrift stores, using coupons, sticking with a $40-per-week grocery budget, and delaying all other purchases which could be put off. These little things might not seem like much on their own, but combined, they were giving us significant traction toward our goal.

Our Monthly Accountability Meetings fueled our drive. We came up with new ways to save and creative ways to add additional income streams. By the second year of saving, we were reaching and *exceeding* our goal every single month. And by the end of two and a half years, we purchased a home—debt-free.

It was an incredible feeling to work hard and reach our goal more than two years earlier than we'd hoped. We know beyond any shadow of a doubt that if we hadn't set the goal in the first place, broken it down into bite-sized pieces, and then kept ourselves accountable by tracking our progress each month, we never would have been able to attain this huge goal in such a short amount of time.

Goals Give You Momentum

Many times, people will say, "I wish we could be where you are financially." And yet if I encourage them to write down goals, they will often just shrug their shoulders in defeat. This always baffles me. The crucial point that they're missing is what I have experienced many times firsthand: when you start working toward your goals, your whole outlook on how you spend your money changes. You feel a sense of satisfaction as you make progress. Saving begets saving, and suddenly you're finding more and more ways to achieve your goal faster than you ever thought possible.

SETTING GOALS WHEN YOU'RE TREADING WATER— OR ALREADY DROWNING

If you're feeling like it's impossible to set goals of any kind because you're just trying to keep clothes on your back, food in your stomach, and the light bill paid, don't be discouraged. As counterintuitive as it might feel at first, now is the perfect time to begin goal setting. Why? Because *you* are the solution to your financial problems. Yes, you can turn things around, starting *today*.

You might be in a major financial mess right now. You might have more credit card debt than you know what to do with and bills that come in faster than you can track. You might be struggling under the load of school loans or an upside-down mortgage. Maybe you're considering filing for bankruptcy. But guess what? You don't have to be stuck unless you choose to be. No matter the state of your finances, there is hope.

The $60 Principle

Here's the key: *small steps can make a big difference.* If you're in serious financial straits, when you sit down to write your goals, you're obviously not going to set a goal to pay off thousands of dollars in debt this year or save to pay cash for a house in the next few years. Instead, you're going to employ the $60 Principle. Your goal will be to save just $60 over the course of the next year. That's $5 each month, or $1.25 a week. Even on the tightest budget, there is almost always a way to scrimp out extra change each week to put toward your financial goal. (If you feel like there's just nothing else you can possibly cut, don't be discouraged. I'll be detailing dozens of ways to save money, stretch your dollars further, and bring in extra income in the chapters that follow.)

You might be thinking, *Why bother? Sixty dollars isn't going to do much for me.* Well, you're right. Sixty dollars isn't going to make a significant dent in paying off debt or buying a house—yet. But the mentality behind saving $60 a year will help you get there.

Inching forward—even at a microscopic rate—is still moving forward. And that's *always* better than standing still or going backward. What we've found to be true time and again is that when you start moving in the right direction financially, you gradually start picking up steam. You discover new and creative ways to lower your expenses. You find extra sources of income. Once again, that *momentum* kicks in. It starts to build, and soon the $5 you're saving each month turns into $10 and then $50. Before you know it, you've paid off a credit card or saved to pay cash for Christmas gifts—just by starting out with a goal of saving $60 a year!

Commit to Short-Term Sacrifice

Getting out of a financial mess will take serious work and short-term sacrifice. You will have to make hard countercultural choices. Your friends will likely not understand. They might even criticize you or call you crazy. Don't let that discourage you.

Focus on your long-term goals and let that motivate you to make short-term sacrifices. It's not easy to make do with what you have instead of going out and buying something new. It's more work to make dinner from scratch than to stop and get carryout. It's hard to say no to things you really want so that you can funnel all your extra money toward digging yourself out of your financial hole. Choosing short-term sacrifice won't be fun or glamorous, but it will be every bit worth it in the long run.

How Eric and Liz Overcame $11,000 in Debt

Eric and Liz decided shortly after marrying in 2005 that they would buy a second car only if they could pay off their debt and save up to pay cash for a second vehicle. Since they had over $11,000 in debt, Liz said, "This seemed like an impossible goal."

They spent the first eighteen months of their marriage just trying to make ends meet. Eric worked his way through school, and all of his paychecks went toward tuition while they subsisted off Liz's salary as a medical secretary. To keep expenses low, they lived in an old trailer and bought most of their groceries with coupons.

When Eric graduated in 2007 and began his career, they made an important decision: instead of upgrading their lifestyle and moving into a nicer apartment, they stayed in their old trailer and put all their extra income toward paying off their debt. By doing this, they were able to pay off $11,000 in just one year!

In 2008, they began looking into purchasing a home. They decided to purchase a home only if they could afford the mortgage payment on Eric's income alone, allowing them to save much of Liz's income. After purchasing their home, they continued to save all of Liz's income, and six months later, they finally had enough saved to buy a second car, a used 2006 Ford Fusion, for $8,000.

Liz says, "I've learned much about patience, contentment, and stewardship in the past few years. Although reluctant about this whole idea at first, I'm glad for the wisdom my husband had financially and am so thankful to not have a car payment."

Liz and Eric never would have paid off $11,000 in debt or been in a position to pay cash for their second vehicle if they had not first set a goal, developed a plan to follow through with that goal, and been willing to make many short-term sacrifices to achieve that goal. When Eric was in school, they didn't have the room in their budget to save much or make much financial traction, but they did what they could—and this put them in a position to pay off their debt and buy a car once their income increased. They also could have ditched their penny-pinching ways once Eric was out of school and they were making a lot more money. Instead, they made hard choices to live well beneath their means and their persistence and perseverance put them in a much better long-term financial situation.

Thinking long-term rather than just living in the moment is the first step toward financial success. Start today by setting goals, breaking them down into bite-sized pieces, making short-term sacrifices, and keeping yourself accountable to stick with it. You just might end up amazed at how much further you'll go when you know where you're headed and you have a rock-solid game plan to get there.

CHAPTER TWO

ARE THE CHAOS AND CLUTTER IN YOUR LIFE KEEPING YOU FROM FINANCIAL SUCCESS?

It's extremely motivating to set goals. But before you put pen to paper to write out your budget, before you start working the cash system I'll detail in chapter 4, before you start cutting coupons, you have to set yourself up for success. And the only way you can do that is to get your life in order.

RULE #2: STREAMLINE YOUR LIFE AND CUT THE CLUTTER

You might think I'm crazy; you might be thinking, *Why are we talking about clutter in my house when I'm $10,000 in debt? Who cares about the stacks of papers on my counter when I'm worried about paying the light bill?*

Here's the thing: you might have great intentions, you

might be able to set inspiring goals, and you may even put together a surefire budget. But if you're drowning in clutter and your days are completely overbooked, implementing any of the money-saving tips in this book is going to be a feat of sheer willpower. Chances are, you'll be hard-pressed to stick to them. When you're already spinning too many plates, adding one more thing to your already-overwhelming to-do list will only leave you dropping some of those spinning plates. So first things first: you need to get a handle on the chaos and clutter in your life.

Karrie and Her Out-of-Control Clutter

Karrie lived in a sea of papers and tub toys. She missed due dates, paid overdraft fees, and threw toys in the trash that got damaged from not being put away. She had a long list of things she could do to improve her family's financial situation, but she never had time to pursue any of them because she was too busy trying to find the baby's socks and get out of the house before the post office closed. The benefits of menu planning and having a filing system were things she knew all too well, but the thought of starting was overwhelming. Her life was so disorganized that she didn't have time to plan ahead, find what she had on hand, or file the looming stacks of papers.

Karrie always spent extra money because she waited until the last minute on everything: she paid for expedited shipping and convenience fees in order to avoid late fees. She even had to schedule an extra optometrist appointment, because she didn't get around to ordering new contacts until just after her prescription expired. Her clutter-induced procrastination caused frustration and stress and brought an added sense of guilt over a messy house, forgotten tasks, and yet another overdraft charge.

Sound familiar? The time to end all the stress over the clutter in your life and free yourself up to focus on your finances is now. Here's a simple plan to get you there. You'll see how it changed everything for Karrie at the end of the chapter.

BECOME THE MASTER OF YOUR MINUTES: ELIMINATING YOUR *PERSONAL* CLUTTER

If you want to get serious about your budget, you have to carve out time for it. It won't just happen. You have to make it happen. And that means you're going to need to restructure your priorities to make time for getting your finances in order.

So many women today struggle with guilt, anxiety, exhaustion, and just generally feeling overwhelmed with life. You have too much on your plate, too many commitments, too much to do and not enough time to breathe, sleep, slow down, and enjoy life. You're killing yourself with overcommitment. It's unhealthy to live life at breakneck speed, and it's likely hurting your relationships and your finances. When you have too much to do, you can't devote the time and energy to what really matters because you're spread too thin and just barely keeping your head above water.

You can't do it all. When you say yes to one thing, you're saying no to another. Now's the time to start saying yes to your financial freedom and peace, and no to those things that are hindering your ability to achieve financial success.

HOW TO STREAMLINE YOUR LIFE AND HAVE TIME FOR WHAT MATTERS

1. Stop Trying to Do It All

One of the biggest factors contributing to women's exhaustion is that they are trying to do too much. We worry about what others will think of us if we don't volunteer for every opportunity, sign up to bake cookies for every bake sale, offer to take a meal to everyone who has a new baby, and accept every committee nomination. Stop the nonsense! Think about it: you're allowing your fear of what others will think of you to steal your joy, time, and sanity.

I want to say something really countercultural. Are you sitting down? Because you probably will want to be before I make this earth-shattering, radically unconventional statement: *It's okay to say no.* There, I said it. You can throw this book across the room if you like. You can be offended and upset with me. But I promise you that until you wrap your head around this concept and start implementing it, you're more than likely going to continue running around feeling frazzled and frantic, stressed and strapped, hurried and harried.

If you want to get your finances in order, you must learn to say no. Not only do you need to learn to say no to overspending and no to buying things you can't afford, but first and foremost you must learn to say no to over-booking your life. You'll never be able to take control of your bank account or make significant traction toward your financial goals if you spend the bulk of your time running around like a chicken with its head cut off.

2. Create a List of Your Personal Priorities

If you know where you want to be in five or ten years, you'll be better able to prioritize how you spend your time. Creating a specific written priorities list instantly helps you to weed through your commitments, eliminating the unimportant from your life so you can keep pressing forward toward what matters most to you.

How to Determine Your Priorities

(Use the spreadsheet on page 190 to help with this exercise.)

- Make a list of everything you're gifted at and love to do.
- Make a second list of things you hope to do in the next five to ten years.
- Make a third list of what five things will be really important to you at the end of your life.
- Take all three lists and see which things automatically overlap and which are most important to you. From there, narrow it down to six to eight personal priorities.

Write down your personal list of six to eight priorities and, just like your written financial goals, keep it in a conspicuous location. Evaluate every opportunity in light of these priorities. For instance, if you'd like to be a published author five years from now, spending your extra time reading well-written books, honing your writing skills, researching publishers, drafting a book proposal, and developing relationships with other published authors and asking them for counsel and advice are all things that will help you move closer toward your goal. If an opportunity arises to meet a publisher or an author, you know it moves you toward your goal. So you'll try to make time for it. If, however, an opportunity to go sky-diving arises, you can say no guiltlessly because it's not on your priority list or likely to propel you closer to your goal.

FOCUS ON YOUR CORE COMPETENCIES

I love the section in *168 Hours: You Have More Time Than You Think* that encourages people to focus on their core competencies. It's pointless to spend too much of your life trying to do something at which you don't excel. Whenever possible, invest your life in what you're truly passionate about and gifted in. You will lead a much more productive and fulfilled life.

---

3. Develop a Time Budget

Once you have your list of priorities, use that as a springboard to develop a Time Budget. The Time Budget concept is one my assistant Amy Lynn Andrews first shared with me when I was feeling overwhelmed with life. I always made these massively impossible to-do lists of everything I wanted to accomplish in a day. I'd never get anywhere near finished and always ended the day feeling frustrated and unproductive. It wasn't that I was unproductive—in reality, I was doing a *lot*! The problem was that I hadn't set a budget for my time.

If you don't tell your money exactly where to go (and I'll be teaching you how to do that in chapter 3), it ends up slipping through your fingers like sand. When you don't have a plan for your money, you won't have much to show for last month's paycheck other than that it's gone. The same is true for time. If you don't have a plan for how you will use your time, you will end up succumbing to, what Charles Hummel aptly called, the "tyranny of the urgent." You'll be busy all day. You'll do lots of things. You'll put out many fires. But you won't make any measurable progress on your goals. And you'll waste precious hours because you didn't have a specific plan for how you were going to spend them.

The Time Budget puts you back in control as the master of your minutes. You will no longer end your day with nothing to show except exhaustion. When you tell your time where to go, not only do you have a lot more time, but you also have a lot more peace and order in your life. This will allow you to be more productive and more energetic. It will propel you toward greater financial and personal success.

"Don't let the urgent take the place of the important in your life."—Charles Hummel[1]

How to Set Up a Time Budget
(Use the worksheet on page 195 to help with this exercise.)

First, start with the time you have. Whether you like it or not, twenty-four hours is all you get. And for many of you, therein lies the reason why you're feeling overwhelmed. You

---

[1] http://www.amazon.com/Tyranny-Urgent-5-Pack/dp/0830865926

are living your life in denial of the fact that you have only twenty-four hours each day and are trying to cram in an extra five hours' worth of work, projects, and activities into time that doesn't exist. No wonder you end the day feeling like you still have ninety-six pressing things left to do; you planned your day forgetting that you only have twenty-four hours to begin with!

People end up overextended financially when they live life spending on credit and pretending to have more money than they do. The same is true with time. You'll soon be burned out and physically depleted if you try to accomplish thirty-six hours' worth of work in a twenty-four-hour day.

Second, block out at least eight hours for sleep. We all know that it's recommended that adults get at least seven to nine hours of sleep, but very few of us actually follow these guidelines. Ironically, burning the midnight oil will not make you more productive. In fact, people who consistently get less than seven hours of sleep are more likely to experience weight issues; be at increased risk for cardiovascular disease, diabetes, and heart disease; exhibit decreased performance and alertness, including memory and cognitive impairment, and have a generally poor quality of life. So put sleep first and you'll live a much more fulfilled, healthy, and energetic life![2]

Next, schedule in two hours of Margin Time. Once you've deducted eight hours for sleep from your twenty-four-hour Time Budget, there's a tendency to want to fill up every

---

[2] http://www.newsweek.com/2010/06/18/the-surprising-toll-of-sleep-deprivation.html; http://articles.mercola.com/sites/articles/archive/2010/08/23/seven-hours—the-magic-number-for-sleep.aspx; http://www.webmd.com/sleep-disorders/guide/important-sleep-habits'; http://www.mayoclinic.com/health/how-many-hours-of-sleep-are-enough/AN01487

single waking moment of the remaining sixteen hours. But if you do that, you'll set yourself up for failure. Why? Because life doesn't ever happen completely according to plan. The phone rings, someone knocks at the door, the baby has a diaper blowout, the washer overflows, you get stuck in traffic. Instead of an unexpected interruption throwing your whole day off, two hours of "Margin Time" scheduled into your day allows you to plan for the unplanned.

Finally, prioritize the remaining fourteen hours. Look at the list of priorities you created earlier and use them as the basis for planning out time blocks for the remaining fourteen hours of your day. You might find that it works best for you to then take these time blocks and assign them to specific times of each day, with some variations depending upon what activities and responsibilities you have on certain days of each week. Or you can just use this Time Budget as a guideline when making your daily to-do list to ensure that you are keeping your priorities in order and not allowing the urgent to overcome the important in your life.

My friend Jessica implemented a Time Budget and has found it to be tremendously helpful to her family. Here's what she says:

"In the past, I felt that I had to have an hour-by-hour schedule because that's what people do. As a homeschool mom of six kids, this was difficult because 'life happens.' I couldn't predict when a diaper would need to be changed or when a child would need extra help. That would inevitably throw off the schedule, and I'd become discouraged because I was behind. A Time Budget is different in the sense that I can allot minutes to a certain task and then grab a block of time when I see it available to get the task done.

"A Time Budget is also different from the standard to-do list, my other past time management system. It helps me feel like I am getting traction. If I put 'laundry' on my list, I'll feel bad if I can't get all the laundry done. But if I know I've budgeted thirty minutes to wash, fold, and put away clothes, that burden of guilt is lifted. I've 'done my duty' for the day even if there's still laundry left to do. Because I 'can't do it all,' a Time Budget helps me recognize my own limitations, helps me see what I am accomplishing, and relieves me of guilt if I don't do it all."

Creating a Time Budget isn't a magic bullet any more than a dollars-and-cents budget is. You have to follow through, you have to pick yourself back up when you fall, you have to constantly reevaluate, tweak, and find something that works. Life is art, not science, so there is always some give and take. But, when you fall off a Time Budget, it's easier to get back into the groove slowly. You can just tackle one particular routine every day and gain momentum until you're back to running smoothly.

STREAMLINE YOUR STUFF: ELIMINATE YOUR *PHYSICAL* CLUTTER

If you want to get your finances in great order, it's near impossible if your home and life are in shambles. How will you keep up with paying the bills if they are buried under mountainous heaps of old mail? How will you know what items to buy when you find a great sale if you don't have a clue what you have on hand? Worse yet is wasting money (and time!) running out to buy something that you have three of but can't locate in your messy home. And if you want to save money by using coupons, you're only setting yourself up for failure and frustration if you have piles and piles of paper clutter littering most flat surfaces in your home. It's time to get the clutter under control and watch how your finances reap the benefits!

HOW TO TAME THE CLUTTER MONSTER

1. Go Through Your House from Top to Bottom

Every six months, I go through our home from top to bottom and ruthlessly eliminate clutter. I clean every nook and cranny, drawer and cupboard, closet and shelf. I evaluate every item. Those things that we no longer need or use I either toss in the trash, give away, or sell. It's pointless for an item to take up space in my house if someone else could use, appreciate, or enjoy it more than I can.

I've found that by doing a complete overhaul of our whole house twice a year, our home never becomes overgrown with clutter. Oh yes, it definitely gets messy and unkempt, but never to a level that is unmanageable.

Going through your house from top to bottom and ruthlessly eliminating clutter might sound like a great idea in theory, but it will happen only if you make it happen. Here's a step-by-step tutorial if this is completely new to you:

Step 1: Make a nonnegotiable appointment with yourself.
Pick a date within the next two weeks that you can block out an entire day (or at least half a day) for turning your home upside down. If your home is in really bad shape, block out an entire weekend to devote to overhauling your home.

I know that many experts suggest doing fifteen minutes of clutter reduction on a daily basis for weeks or months until you've cleaned out your home. This might work for some, but I think it's better if you just get it all over with in one big sweep. You'll feel better, your house will show immediate improvement, and you won't be dragging it out for months on end.

Step 2: Remove all distractions. Going through your home like this is not an easy task—especially if you've never done it before. You need to mute all distractions so you can focus wholeheartedly on the task at hand. If you have children, hire a sitter or leave them with Grandma for the day. Turn off the TV and computer. Plan a very simple dinner. Don't answer the door or phone. You have a job to do, don't let anything or anyone keep you from it!

Step 3: Set up a system for clutter removal. Get five boxes, tubs, or trash bags and label them "Trash," "Get Rid Of," "File," "Put Away," and "I'm Not Sure." Have a clipboard with two sheets of paper, one titled "Things to Do" and the other, "Furniture to Get Rid Of."

Step 4: Set the timer and dive in. Set a timer for thirty minutes and start with the first room that you walk into when you enter your home:

- Scan the room quickly and see if all the furniture is serving a purpose. If not, put it on the clipboard list of "Furniture to Get Rid Of." You'll deal with this later.
- Gather up all the trash and put it in the "Trash" bag.
- Look at every flat surface and put anything that doesn't belong in the room in your "Get Rid Of," "File," "Put Away," or "I'm Not Sure" boxes.
- Go through every closet, drawer, and cupboard. Don't worry about deep cleaning right now, your main job is to remove clutter from your home. Ask yourself the five questions about clutter (see page 33) as you analyze each item and decide whether to keep it or toss it. You don't have all day to be in one room; this is a race against the clock. Work as quickly as you can. Don't dawdle; don't be wishy-washy. Attack the clutter with vengeance!
- As you are going through each room, you'll probably notice in-depth projects you want to tackle (e.g. paint a wall, replace a blind, clean the stain off the couch or carpet, set up an organizational system for your DVDs, etc.). Instead of getting distracted and starting in on one or more of these projects, just write it down on your "Projects to Tackle" list. After you've finished clearing out the clutter in your home, pull out this list and assign these projects to later free afternoons or evenings on your calendar.
- Once your thirty minutes is up, stop and take ten minutes to throw out the trash in the "Trash" bag, put away anything that can be quickly put away in another room from the "Put Away" box, file the items from the "File"

box, and put the room back into presentable order if there are things still out.

- Set the timer for another thirty minutes and move onto the next room. Repeat the above steps.

- After you have worked through your whole house in the above manner, decide whether you need to take another day to do another room-by-room overhaul to eliminate more clutter. If so, write it down on your calendar and don't let anything keep you from it. I promise it will be worth it!

- Once you've gone through your home from top to bottom, spend an hour or two going through your "I Don't Know" and "Get Rid Of" boxes. Evaluate each item to decide whether you want to keep it, throw it out, give it away, or sell it (see page 35 for "Three Ways to Turn Your Clutter into Cash").

- Finally, take your list of "Furniture to Get Rid Of" and decide when and how you'll be getting rid of these items.

Once your home is in good shape and you feel like you've pared down almost all of the non-essential items just taking up extra space, then you are ready to move onto the next step—staying on top of the clutter on an ongoing basis.

Tip: If you need some extra accountability, ask a non–pack-rat friend to help you go through your home. She's unattached to your stuff and can help you think more objectively. Need even more motivation? Consider taking before and after pictures and posting them on your blog or Facebook page!

FIVE QUESTIONS TO ASK YOURSELF
ABOUT CLUTTER

1. **Do I need this item?** *Need* is the keyword here. If you could live without the item, then you probably don't. I'm not saying you should only have two outfits and one pair of shoes, but objectively considering how much of the stuff you have is truly essential can help change your perspective.

2. **Do I use this item regularly?** If you use something only once every six months, get rid of it. Christmas decorations are exempt, but if you have a food dehydrator lurking in a basement corner that you've only used once in the last ten years, you either need to pull it out and start using it or find a better home for it—preferably someone *else's* home.

3. **Do I like this item?** Sometimes it is easy to keep clutter just because we always have. It becomes a part of our home without us ever examining whether it is a useful part or something we like and use. If it's doing nothing for you and you don't even like it in the first place, pitch it!

4. **Is this item taking up space I don't have?** Many people feel like they need a bigger home for all their stuff, but most people just need less stuff. When my husband and I first got married, we spent the first six months living in a one-bedroom apartment with one closet. We made use of all our available room, from under the bed to under the bathroom sink, and learned an invaluable lesson: the less space you have, the less stuff you need.

5. **Could I bless someone else with this item?** One of my favorite ways to "dispose" of items I no longer love, need, or use is to share them with someone who will! Not only do I get the item off my hands, but I bless someone else in the process—and likely save them money, too! Now, I am not advocating that you go dump ten bags of junk on your friend's doorstep, but if you know your friend could use some diapers and you have half a box that your son outgrew, stop letting them take up space in the nursery and ask your friend if she'd like them!

2. Stay on Top of the Clutter Aggressively

I wish I could tell you that once you go through your house from top to bottom and ruthlessly eliminate clutter, you'll never need to worry about clutter again. Unfortunately, that's not how it works. Clutter is like a pesky weed that must be sprayed and uprooted constantly, lest it start taking over again.

But there is hope! If you're willing to be aggressive and keep at it, you can successfully win the battle against clutter in your home. Here are three easy ways to keep the clutter at bay:

- **Set Up Ongoing Clutter Boxes.** Designate a section of a closet or storage room for clutter boxes. Instead of tripping over an item, thinking a dozen times, *We really should get rid of that ugly wall hanging*, just take it straight out to the clutter box to store until your next garage sale, trip to the thrift store, or eBay listing blitz. Not only is the clutter now out of your way, but it's so much easier to gather up and get rid of when it's all in a designated spot.

I love to have garage sales, so I have designated Garage Sale tubs in our garage that I add to gradually over a six-month period. Twice a year, I join forces with family members and we have a big multifamily garage sale. Since I already have a number of items set aside, it doesn't take long to pull my stuff together and price it. (See the Appendix for more tips and tricks for having a successful garage sale.)

If garage sales aren't your thing, then you can either sell your items (see below for "Three Ways to Turn Your Clutter into Cash") or drop off your clutter boxes at a local thrift store or shelter every few months. If you itemize your taxes, you can claim this as a deduction—and you don't even have to mess with running a garage sale.

THREE WAYS TO TURN YOUR
CLUTTER INTO CASH

Craigslist: If you live in a large metropolis, your local Craigslist is likely hopping with potential buyers. Take good pictures, use descriptive words, include only your email address (there are weirdos on the internet; no need to give them your home phone number!), and price your item reasonably. Chances are, finding a buyer will be fairly simple. Best of all? If the item doesn't sell, you're out nothing but time and effort. Craigslist is a great place to sell almost *anything*, but I'd especially recommend using it for selling exercise equipment, appliances, and baby items.

eBay: eBay may be a great option, but it is so well known that the market is often saturated. Before listing items on eBay, do a search to see if an item you are considering selling on eBay is actually *selling*. If there are dozens of listings of your item and very few bids, you're probably going to do better selling your item elsewhere.

I have had success with selling items as "lots" as opposed to individually. This is a quick way to get rid of many items at once. It will save you the time and energy of taking pictures and listing each thing separately and you'll likely get more bidders. Make sure that you do have a few hot sellers in the lot, use descriptive keywords in your title and listing, and include at least one or two high-quality photos of your items.

Consignment Stores: Consignment stores normally specialize in selling name-brand used clothing. Children's consignment stores also sell baby items, maternity clothes, toys, and more. There are at least one or two available in most areas. All consignment stores have their own rules and guidelines, but most either pay you upfront in cash or in store credit. Or they'll display the items in their store and then pay you a percentage of the selling price if your item sells.

Depending on the items, condition, and brand, this could be an excellent opportunity. I'd recommend calling around to local consignment stores to see what their rules and guidelines for accepting items are and how much they pay.

- **When You Get Something New, Get Rid of Something Old.** This is a simple rule, but it works incredibly well. When you bring new items into your home, require yourself to get rid of the same number of items. For instance, when you get a new pair of shoes, choose one pair to get rid of. When your children have a birthday and get new toys, have them choose the same number of old toys to get rid of. Without much effort, this rule keeps clutter from prolific breeding in the closets behind your back.

- **Institute a No-Pile Rule.** When you allow a small pile to start, it grows—without any effort. Soon it can get out of hand, becoming overwhelming, fostering disorganization, and keeping you from finding what you need. Because of this, we have a No-Pile Rule at our house. Except for my husband's dresser and the laundry pile, we don't allow piles to start or fester. Here's how we accomplish this:

  » *Go through the mail and all incoming papers immediately.* Instead of shuffling paper from place to place, deal with it immediately. File what needs to be filed, write any dates you need to remember on the calendar, and toss what needs to be tossed.

  » *Throw out the sales fliers and catalogs.* Unless you are 150 percent sure you are going to need to consult a flier or catalog for planning your grocery shopping trip or for online shopping within the next week, throw it out. In most cases, you can get all the information from sales fliers and catalogs online. If there's a coupon you want to keep or think you'll use, stick it in a file or tub designated for coupons. (We'll talk more about how to set up a coupon organizational system later; for now, just having a designated tub, envelope, or drawer for these will work.)

» *Create a simple filing system for bills.* If possible, I strongly encourage you to set up online bill pay. It will save you time, paper, and stamps. But whether or not you set up online bill pay, you still need a system for saving and filing bills, invoices, and receipts. So keep it simple: have one file for bills needing to be paid, one file for bills already paid, and a file for important papers you need to keep. An inexpensive file box and filing folders are all you need. As you think of other files that would be helpful to have, add them to your system.

» *Have a box for keeping special cards, toss the rest.* This might sound terribly ruthless, but if someone just signed his name to a Hallmark card, there really isn't a whole host of reasons to hang on to it, you know? Unless it's someone who has never sent you a card before or you have some other deeply sentimental reason, let go of the guilt and open the trash can!

As much as possible, remove coffee tables, end tables, or other furniture that only seems to collect piles of clutter. You're less apt to create piles if you don't have easily accessible places for them to build up.

How Karrie Cleared Her Clutter and Overhauled Her Budget

Remember Karrie, my frazzled friend who was totally unorganized and paying—literally—for it? Here's what happened when she got her personal and physical clutter under control.

Karrie knew things needed to change, so she picked a week to start, cleared her schedule of all commitments, and planned simple meals for that week. She took a day to walk through the house and identify specific clutter problem areas as well as those that needed storage solutions. Then she assigned each problem area a different day of her "organization week."

When the big day came to start on the first area, she emptied it and sorted every item to either be thrown away, sold, donated, or reorganized back into the space. Once her household clutter was under control, she then tackled how to schedule her days so that she could stay organized instead of letting things lapse back into disarray.

Karrie has so much more peace and order in her life now that she's gotten her clutter and her schedule in control. Best of all, she's saving so much more money than she ever could have when she was disorganized. She says, "Birthdays and events don't sneak up on me anymore. I plan ahead and get great deals on gifts and other things we need to purchase for events, instead of rushing out and paying full price for something at the last minute. I no longer pay late fees or buy items to replace things that were lost or broken when they weren't put away properly. I save on gas money by planning ahead to avoid extra trips to town and by not always being late and in a hurry. I make sure to stay under 60 mph, which burns considerably less gas. Also, I don't ever need to go back home to get something I forgot, because when planning my trips ahead of time, I lay out everything I'll need for that trip, as I go through my list of errands.

"Living frugally is not overwhelming, and I don't get burned out. I enjoy clipping coupons, planning shopping trips, and planning meals, because my coupon system is organized and simple and I have a day of the week set aside for clipping and organizing my coupons. I'm still just as *busy* as I was before, but I'm much more *productive* and much more relaxed. Things don't catch me off-guard like they used to, and I can plan ahead for expenses on my calendar, *and* in my budget."

Remember that while you might want to jump right into making a budget, using coupons, and getting great deals online, if your home and life are not in order, you are just going to make things harder for yourself and likely end up frustrated and overwhelmed. Do yourself a favor: don't go on to the next chapter until you've carefully followed the steps outlined in this chapter. Not only will you have more time and energy, you'll be ready to jump into transforming your finances with zest!

FIVE WAYS BEING ORGANIZED
SAVES YOU MONEY

1. You'll be able to plan a weekly menu and you'll already have the ingredients on hand so that you're not scrambling to figure out something for dinner at the last minute. This saves you time, sanity, and countless unnecessary trips through the drive-through lane.

2. You'll be able to buy gifts for upcoming birthdays and holidays when you find a great deal online or in-store instead of waiting until the last minute and having to buy something at full price. As an added benefit, you'll likely be able to put more time and thought into a meaningful gift rather than just throwing something together at the last minute.

3. You'll have the time to clip coupons and buy extras of items when they are free or at rock-bottom prices, potentially saving you hundreds of dollars each month on your grocery bill.

4. You'll be able to plan ahead and pay bills on time and return DVDs to the movie store and books to the library so that you avoid late fees and overdue fines.

5. You can find what you own. This saves you a lot of time looking for misplaced items, plus it keeps you from spending money to replace items you can't find.

CHAPTER THREE

GIVE YOURSELF AN INSTANT RAISE WITHOUT INCREASING YOUR TAKE-HOME PAY

When I talk about setting financial goals and saving up and paying cash for things, I'm often met with resistance. "But you don't understand!" people say, and they shake their heads in disbelief. "There's no way we could set financial goals or save up and pay cash because we're barely keeping our heads above water as it is. We're doing good if we're able to pay for groceries and the electric bill!"

I have great news for you: if you implement the steps outlined in this chapter, you very likely will have more than enough money to pay for all your basic necessities. In fact, you will probably find you have some leftover to save and give. What I'm about to share with you just might change the course of your finances—for *life*.

Have you ever bemoaned the fact that if only you had more money, you could get your finances straightened out?

Well, I have found a proven method to give yourself an instant raise—without actually *making* more money. Sound too good to be true? It's not. It's worked for hundreds of thousands of people, and it can work for you, too.

What's the secret formula? It's called a *budget*. It's probably not what you were wanting to hear, but, believe me, it works. I dare you to take the three-month challenge and see if it makes any difference in your finances.

How Audrienne and Matt Overcame a $358 Monthly Deficit with a Budget

"After my husband and I got married, we never stuck with a budget. We only made $30,000 per year, so we felt like we were too poor to budget. We thought we were just spending only what we needed, and that was the best we could do. We didn't even bother to track our spending.

"We kept hearing from others how important it was to have a budget, but we weren't convinced it would do us any good. Finally, with our second baby on the way, we decided to get serious and actually try setting up a budget. To our dismay, we realized that if we were to fund all of our budget categories, we'd be going over our monthly income by $358! I took this as a challenge and began playing with the numbers, seeing if we could live on less. In doing this, I realized there were a number of small changes we could make that would lower our monthly expenditures and close that $358 gap.

"By living on a budget and consistently tracking every

penny we spent, for the first time in years, we've been able to pay all of our bills without having a deficit. Plus, we've had enough money left over to pay off our debt, and start putting away money into savings every month. Budgeting has changed our lives!"

RULE #3: SET UP A REALISTIC, WORKABLE BUDGET

If you're completely new to budgeting, don't make it more complicated than it needs to be. In fact, I'm going to go against what most financial advisors will tell you and encourage you *not* to start with a full-blown budget that lists every category, expenditure, and line item. Sure, by going this route, you won't see the same kind of immediate savings and change as you would if you overhauled your finances tonight and created a to-the-penny budget. However, you'll make things much easier on yourself, you'll be gradually shifting your habits in the right direction and, long-term, you'll see lasting and significant changes.

Three Months to a Realistic, Workable Budget

First Month: The Food Budget

The easiest area to start with when it comes to budgeting is your grocery budget because—let's face it—everyone has to eat. It's also one of the easiest areas from which to cut down your expenditures significantly.

To determine a workable grocery budget, look back over

your grocery expenses for the last few months and average out what you usually spent each week. Then multiply that number by four. That's the monthly grocery budget you're going to start with. For instance, if you normally spend somewhere around $200 per week at the grocery store, then you'll allot $800 per month for groceries and household products.

If you don't have any of the grocery receipts from the last few months, don't panic! A good ballpark figure to go with is $40 per person per week for groceries and household products (cleaning supplies, makeup, hygiene products, over-the-counter medicines, etc.). This number might vary depending upon your family size, your location, your family's appetites, and food preferences. In addition, if you have food allergies or sensitivities, those will also play a major role in how much you'll need to spend on groceries. Don't stress about the number, though. The point is to just set a food budget and stick with it. If you've never had a budget, this one change can be a huge step in the right direction.

I'll teach you all sorts of tricks for lowering your grocery bill in chapter 6, but for now, start with a budget that is manageable. The last thing you need to do is set yourself up for failure by creating a grocery budget that is way too low.

Once you've determined what your food budget will be (and it's up to you whether you include enough to cover eating out or just grocery shopping trips), withdraw the full amount for the grocery budget in cash for the month. Put this amount in an envelope and take out the weekly allotment each week to spend at the store.

How Cambria Changed the Way She Thought About Money by Setting Up a Grocery Budget

"A few months ago, I gave myself the challenge to stick to a $50-per-week grocery budget for our family of three. We are in medical school, and every little penny counts, so I was determined to stay on budget. It's been a challenge because I used to spend $550 to $600 per month on groceries and thought people who had budgets and used coupons just needed to get a life! I had always said that I'd rather *make* money than save money. But the funny thing is, until I started sticking to a budget for our groceries, we were just going further and further into debt.

"Gaining control over this one area of our finances has helped me realize I can be in control of all of our money. I am so glad that I've finally seen the 'financial light' and am now committed to keep all our finances in check."

Why Cash?

If you're not used to using cash, you might be balking right now at the thought of withdrawing a big lump sum and using it for your groceries over the next four weeks. I understand that cash gets a bad rap. It can be lost or stolen. It doesn't earn you any points like a credit card does. And it can burn a hole in your pocket and beg to be spent.

However, despite the arguments against using cash, the beauty of using cash instead of swiping a card is that you can't go over budget. It forces you to stick with your budget because, when the money's gone, it's gone. If you use up your full amount of your monthly grocery money the first two and a half weeks, you won't be able to buy any more groceries until the next month. This motivates you to evaluate purchases carefully so that you don't run out of money before the month is over.

Don't be alarmed if you really struggle with this the first month you try it. It takes time and practice to learn to pace yourself and make the money in the envelope last for at least as long as it's supposed to. But stick with it and you'll soon get a much better handle on staying within the budget. And you'll probably start looking for ways to spend less and stretch the dollars you have further!

If, after a few months, you feel like the number you've determined just isn't working for you, change it. There's no rule that says you can't tweak your budget once you've created it. In fact, I encourage you to re-evaluate your budget on a regular basis to see if you need to raise or lower amounts in different categories. As your circumstances, needs, and priorities ebb and flow, so should your budget.

"When I first started budgeting, I decided to make a food budget, but I didn't use cash. I just logged my expenditures on paper and continued to use my credit card or debit card. It took about four months for me to admit that I was failing this way. When I switched to a cash-only food budget, we went from spending over $800 a month on food to spending $550 a month on food. Using cash really makes a difference!"

—Donna S., MoneySavingMom.com reader,
mother of five

Second Month: The Bare-bones Budget

After a month of following a food budget, hopefully you should feel like you are starting to get a handle on staying within your grocery budget. If so, it's time to move on to the next step: the Bare-bones Budget. This covers your basic necessities, the things you need to survive: food, basic utilities (electricity, trash, water, gas, phone service), shelter, and transportation.

You've already got one need taken care of: food. Now you just need to determine how much to budget for basic utilities, shelter, and transportation. It isn't difficult, especially if you stick with four budget categories that cover all of these.

Bare-bones Budget Spreadsheet Categories

(See page 199 for a spreadsheet you can fill out.)

Food

  Groceries

  Eating Out

Basic Utilities

  Trash

  Water

  Electricity

  Gas

  Landline Phone Service

  Cell Phone Service

Shelter

  Mortgage/Rent

  Homeowner's Insurance/Renter's Insurance

> *Transportation*
> Car Payment #1
> Car Payment #2
> Public Transportation
> Gas
> Auto Repairs

Basic Utilities

To determine how much you should budget for utility costs, add up your utility bills from the last year and then divide this number by twelve. You should come up with a pretty accurate amount to budget (if you've moved in the last few months, you'll need to just give an educated guess and then tweak this number after a few months). Set this money aside each month in your checking account specifically for your utilities and only touch it when you need to pay your utility bills. You won't always use the full amount, but you'll want to save whatever is left over for months when you have higher bills.

Shelter

Your rent or mortgage payment is covered under the Shelter heading, as is any renter's insurance, home owner's insurance, property taxes, or other must-pay bills related to your housing. You probably know these costs already, but in case you don't, a quick look at your previous rent or mortgage payment can clue you in. Typically, you pay for insurance once a year, but you can go ahead and divide the amount by twelve and then set aside 1/12th of it each month. At the end of the year, you'll have the amount saved up and you can just write the insurance check, no sweat.

Transportation

This category covers your car payment(s), gas costs, auto up-keep, and any public transportation or parking fees. In order to determine how much you should set aside, calculate how much you usually spend on average for transportation costs each month. Your car payment (if you have one) should be easy to figure out, but gas and auto expenses can be a bit more tricky. You can look at previous gas station receipts and/or auto expense receipts. Or you can estimate what seems a reasonable amount and then tweak this at the end of the month if it was too much or too little. It will normally take you at least three to six months to really decide on a good figure to set aside for auto and gas expenses, and this number will fluctuate with changing gas prices.

We've found that it's easiest to pay for gas with cash. It's not as easy as paying at the pump (and might be impractical if you usually fill up with three kids in the car!), but it helps you keep better track of how much you're spending if you withdraw a set amount for gas at the beginning of each pay period, stick it in an envelope marked "gas," and then pay for your gas expenses with this cash only.

HOW TO SET UP A BARE-BONES BUDGET

Once you've calculated how much you'll be budgeting for each of the Bare-bones Budget categories each month (if you are paid bi-monthly, see page 53 for details on how to divvy up your paycheck), take out the gas, groceries, and eating-out money in cash as soon as you get your paycheck. Put these in designated envelopes, keep them in a safe place, and access them only when you're going to be spending the money. Do not allow yourself to use these funds for anything else—no matter how tempting it may be!

For the other budget categories, set up a separate checking account and deposit the total lump sum of what you need to cover them each month as soon as you receive your paycheck. While having a separate checking account for these categories might seem like an extra step, it will make it much easier to keep track of your expenses, practice sticking with a budget, and see exactly where your money is going, and will prepare you for the next step of doing a Full-fledged Budget.

You can use the spreadsheet at the back of the book to set up your Bare-bones Budget, you can create your own spreadsheet, or you can use an online money tracker like Mint.com. Whatever you do, it's not enough just to set up the budget, you also have to follow it, and this means tracking all your expenses from the Bare-bones Budget to ensure you aren't going over budget. This does not need to be a complicated. Keep it simple. The last thing you need to do is create some exhaustive process that will leave you, well, exhausted!

What I love about the Bare-bones Budget is that it allows you to pare down your expenses to the basics. You'll still be spending money outside of these four categories (we'll get to the Full-fledged Budget in just a few paragraphs), but by breaking it down to your necessities, you're able to realize how little you can live on if you had to.

Think with me for a moment. If you have a comfortable shelter to live in, running water and lights, a car to drive, and food in your belly, life isn't all that bad. Sure, you might have a pile of debt, but if you take care of the bare bones first, nobody is going hungry and you will survive.

WHAT IF MY FIRST PAYCHECK WON'T COVER ALL THE BARE-BONES BUDGET CATEGORIES?

If you add up all of the Bare-bones Budget categories and your first paycheck of the month won't cover the sum total, you will need to set priorities based upon what's due when and fill the categories accordingly. For example, if your housing payment is due at the beginning of the month and your utilities aren't due until the end of the month, you'll want to prioritize your housing payment for the first paycheck of the month and then take out your utility payments from the second paycheck of the month.

Once you have stuck with the Bare-bones Budget for a month, you are ready to move on to a Full-fledged Budget. Congratulations! Now is where you'll really begin to reap the fruit of your hard efforts!

Third Month: The Full-fledged Budget

You already have a handle on budgeting now that you've had a Food Budget and a Bare-bones Budget. It's time to step it up a notch and create a Full-fledged Budget. Don't be intimidated. Your goal here is just to tell every dollar where to go. If you do nothing else when it comes to finances—if you never clip a coupon, never shop sales, never take your lunch to work, and never buy used—but you follow a Full-fledged Budget, you'll benefit a great deal. In fact, you might find you have an extra few hundred or even an extra thousand dollars each month. That's certainly nothing to sneeze at!

How to Set Up a Full-fledged Budget

If you're completely new to budgeting, realize that a workable Full-fledged Budget is not going to happen overnight. It will likely take you at least three months to feel comfortable with it. The first two months, you'll probably overfund some categories and underfund others. You might even completely overlook a whole category you should include. That's okay!

This is a learning process that will get better and easier as time goes on. However, keep in mind as I mentioned earlier that a budget should never be considered "set in stone"; a good budget gets tweaked and reworked on a monthly or semiannual basis as your needs and expenses change.

1. Write down all of your monthly expenses using the list below as a guide. If you don't know an exact amount, give an educated guess. (See page 200 for a spreadsheet you can fill out.)

   Ideas for Budget Categories
   Charitable Gifts
   Savings
   Emergency Fund
   Retirement Fund
   College Fund

House Fund

Car Fund

Baby Fund

Housing
    Mortgage/Rent
    Real Estate Taxes
    Homeowner's/Renter's Insurance
    Repairs/Remodeling

Utilities
    Electricity
    Water
    Gas
    Landline Phone
    Cell Phone
    Trash
    Cable
    Internet

Food/Household Items
    Groceries
    Eating Out
    Household Products/Toiletries
    Cosmetics

Transportation
    Car Payment #1
    Car Payment #2
    Gas
    Repairs
    Car Insurance
    License and Taxes

Health and Medical
   Disability Insurance
   Health Insurance
   Life Insurance
   Doctor's Visits
   Dental Work
   Optometrist
   Contacts/Glasses
   Medications

Debt
   Credit Card #1
   Credit Card #2
   Credit Card #3
   Line of Credit
   Student Loan #1
   Student Loan #2
   Other

Personal/Recreation

Clothing

Child Care/Babysitting

Hair Care

Education

School Tuition/Supplies

Subscriptions

Gifts

Miscellaneous

Vacation

Entertainment

Other

"Each year when I receive my home insurance renewal notice, I call the company and ask if they will work with me to come up with a better rate. I have done this each year since buying a home and have always saved at least $100 off the quoted rate."

—Christina, MoneySavingMom.com reader

---

2. Determine how much you should allot for each category on a monthly basis.

This doesn't have to be perfect. The Bare-bones Budget will need lots of refining. Start with your best estimate and tweak it at your monthly Budget Meeting if you find it's too low or too high.

A WORD OF CAUTION: GIVE YOURSELF SOME WIGGLE ROOM!

Don't be unrealistic. If you're going to stick with a budget for the long haul, you need to allow yourself some wiggle room. In fact, I'm going to go so far as to say that it is a healthy thing to budget for splurges. That might seem to fly in the face of frugal living, but I promise you'll thank me for it. You see, if you create a budget that is so bare-bones it doesn't allow you any breathing room, you'll soon suffocate.

In the long run, not saving as aggressively as you had hoped because you have occasional budgeted splurges may be preferable to going so hard-core for six months that you burn out on being a tightwad and blow hundreds (or thousands) on a spending spree. Prevent this from the get-go by planning for specific regular strategic splurging.

3. Add up all your monthly expenses and subtract them from your take-home (net) pay.

Hopefully, you'll end up with more income than expenses. In this case, determine what items you'd like to save for or budget areas you can increase. Focus your extra money on paying off debt first and then toward savings goals, rather than just blowing it on something that won't benefit you long term.

4. If your expenses are more than your income, decide what you can cut out or lower (see page 59 for ideas for lowering many of your monthly expenses).

Consider eliminating things such as subscriptions, cable television, and gym memberships. Yes, it might hurt, but billions of people have survived for centuries without cable and magazines. And workout videos cost a fraction of many monthly gym rates. Limit dining out and entertainment costs if these are eating a big chunk of your budget. Negotiate lower rates on your utility bills, see if you can lower your insurance premiums, and by all means, pay off your debt. The sooner you can free yourself from the bondage of debt, the sooner you can live on less!

As you probably discovered with the Food Budget and Bare-bones Budget, a Full-fledged Budget takes work. It won't just happen. But if you commit to creating it and then sticking with it, it will change your world—and your financial situation.

TEN DRASTIC MEASURES TO LOWER YOUR EXPENSES BY AT LEAST $600 OR MORE PER MONTH

If you've done your budget and came up short by a few hundred or a few thousand dollars each month, you need to do some serious cutting of your expenses. Remember, these are just short-term sacrifices to get you in a better financial position for the long term. I wouldn't recommend doing some of these things lifelong, but if you are in a real bind, here are ten ways to significantly cut your expenses:

1. **Downsize Your Home.** If you are renting, do the math to see if moving to a smaller house or apartment might be worth the effort. If you're bursting at the seams as it is, follow the steps outlined in chapter 2 to streamline your life and get rid of clutter. Maybe you'll find you can actually get by with a smaller living space, or at least you'll figure out that you don't necessarily need to get a bigger place. The less stuff you have, the less space you need to comfortably live. *Possible savings: $150 or more each month.*

2. **Become a Single-car Family.** This won't work for everyone, but it's worth considering long and hard if there's a way you can eliminate all but one vehicle for at least a short time period. Calculate how much you'd save if you got rid of one (or more) of your vehicles and then

brainstorm if there's a way you could make it work. An added benefit of sharing a vehicle with your spouse is that you will stay home more, which usually results in spending less money. *Possible savings: $100 or more each month.*

3. **Stop Eating Out.** Restaurants are great, but they are expensive. You can often make a week's worth of simple meals for the cost of a single dinner out at a sit-down restaurant. If you feel like you can't survive without eating out occasionally, see page 146 for some ideas on how to eat out for half the price or less. *Possible savings: $100 or more each month.*

4. **Get Rid of Cable.** You can live without cable! People have done it for centuries and been no worse for it. In fact, I think that incessant watching of mindless television is only sucking out our brains and creativity. See page 151 for cable alternatives that are free. *Possible savings: $25 or more each month.*

5. **Cancel All Subscriptions and Memberships.** No matter how much you love that magazine subscription, Netflix account, or gym membership, if you can't afford to pay your utility bill, the extra memberships have got to go. See pages 165 for some free and very inexpensive alternatives to memberships. *Possible savings: $15 or more each month.*

6. **Cut the Bells and Whistles on Your Phone.** If you have a fancy cell phone with all the bells and whistles, get rid of it and replace it with a pay-as-you-go phone plan. Cut the extras on your landline or consider eliminating it altogether.

See page 164 for less expensive landline alternatives. *Possible savings: $15 or more each month.*

7. **Eat More Meatless Meals.** This is drastic for some people, I know, but if you're desperate, it's a fantastic way to save a good chunk of change each week. You'll typically pay at least $2 to $4 for just the meat you serve at a meal. Switch to simple, inexpensive vegetarian meals at least two or three times per week (vegetable soup, beans and rice, bean burritos, pancakes and eggs for dinner, etc.) and pocket the savings. *Possible savings: $35 or more each month.*

8. **Quit Using Your Dryer.** Your dryer is one of the most expensive appliances to run. Invest in a simple outdoor clothesline or indoor clothes rack for drying your clothes. *Possible savings: $15 or more each month.*

9. **Adjust Your Thermostat.** Turning your thermostat up or down by two or three degrees can have a pretty significant impact on your heating and cooling bills. You can also save approximately 10 percent by turning your thermostat back by 10 to 15 degrees for eight hours (overnight).[3] Invest in a programmable thermostat to automate this. *Possible savings: $25 or more per month.*

10. **Plan a Menu and Use Coupons.** Committing to spend an extra hour each week menu planning and matching store sales with coupons can yield a significant savings on your grocery bill. See page 125 for more details on how to lower your grocery bill. *Possible savings: $125 or more each month.*

---

[3] http://www.energysavers.gov/your_home/space_heating_cooling/index.cfm/mytopic=12720}

"We pay our insurance premiums in full, rather than make monthly payments. We get a discount for doing this, plus we can earn a little bit of interest in our savings account while we wait for the bill to come due. We take the total premium for a year and divide it by twelve months, and deposit that amount into our savings account each month. Since we do this for our car insurance, renter's insurance, flood insurance, and life insurance policies, the savings really add up."

—Kacie, MoneySavingMom.com reader

BUT WHAT IF I HAVE A VARIABLE INCOME?

Many people today do not have a fixed amount that they bring home each month. Whether you are self-employed, work on a commission, or work odd hours, it's entirely possible to budget on a variable income. In fact, for much of our married life we've not had a fixed income.

To budget on a variable income, create a Bare-bones Budget with all the essentials from the list above. Fund these first each month. Then, if there is money left over, set aside some of it toward savings for leaner months and the rest toward nonessentials. If there's nothing left over after funding the Bare-bones Budget, you just won't save anything that month, and you won't buy anything nonessential. I've found that you can usually make do with what you have for at least a few months, if not longer.

In our house, we have a list of extra savings goals we're working toward. We fund them with our leftover money, in order of priority. On the months where we do really well, we're able to save significant amounts toward these savings goals. On other months, we can't always cover all our extra savings goals—and that's okay, since none of them are essentials.

"As a single woman, it can be difficult to maintain a balanced attitude toward finances. It's easy to either blow a lot of money (because there's no one asking me where it goes) or be so stingy that I simply don't give or spend money. I don't have a spouse to balance my tendency to swing to one extreme or the other, so that's one of my favorite reasons for a using a cash budget: it helps me maintain a balanced attitude. When I make a budget, I'm giving myself permission to spend that money. Creating a budget helps to keep me from wasting money— and having money in designated envelopes that I've given myself 'permission' to spend makes so I don't have to be stingy or feel guilty spending money."

—Bethany, MoneySavingMom.com reader

THREE COMMON BUDGETING EXCUSES AND WHY I DON'T BUY THEM

Excuse #1: "I can't stand the thought of having a budget. It sounds so restrictive." You know what's a whole lot more restrictive than knowing where your money is going and how much you have to spend? Not knowing where your money is going, running out of money, and never being able to get ahead. If you don't tell your money where to go, it usually just disappears each month with little to show for it. Without a budget, you will probably never make the financial progress you want to make because you lack the purpose and plan to do so.

Wouldn't you rather be in charge of your money, telling it where to go and when to go there, and knowing that you have enough to cover all your needs—and, hopefully, some wants, too? A budget will do just that. Yes, you have to stick with it and not overspend, but instead of it being restrictive, we've found it to be just the opposite: it's *freeing*!

You see, if you have $35 each week in your Eating Out budget category, you can have fun using that without having to worry that your delicious dinner out might keep you from being able to pay your electric bill next week. Why? Because you've already set aside money for your electric bill in your Utilities budget category in your checking account.

Excuse #2: "I wish I could implement a budget, but my husband would never go for that." Dealing with a difficult spouse is hard. And, unfortunately, there are no pat answers because each situation is different. I'd encourage you to sit down and discuss your desire to implement a budget with your husband, if he's willing to. Ask him how he feels about your finances and what areas he'd like to see changed. Ask him how you can change. (And listen willingly to what he has to say. If you're not willing to change, then certainly you can't expect him to change, either!)

It's possible your husband is almost 100 percent to blame

for your money problems. But I'd give a good guess that you both have some areas you need to work on. Showing him that you're willing to work on things along with him will probably go a long way toward helping you both get on the same page about finances. If you can't sit down and discuss this together, there may be deeper issues that need to be addressed through formal marriage counseling.

Excuse #3: "A budget is so complicated. I just don't have time for it with how busy my life is." Frankly, I don't think you have time to not know where your money is going—unless you want to live all your life in paycheck-to-paycheck mode, never get ahead, and spend your retirement in the poorhouse! And truthfully, a budget can be as complex or simple as you choose to make it. It could be as simple as a lined notebook with handwritten categories. Or you could make complex spreadsheets on the computer with formulas. It's up to you.

The point is to make a budget that works for you and then to work the budget. The best of intentions won't get you anywhere unless you also have follow-through. You can have the most beautifully laid out budget in the world, but if you don't use it, nothing will change.

"Four years ago, our family's income was decreased by 63 percent. We had never felt like we'd needed a budget before, but this motivated us to create our very first budget. By using coupons to cut our grocery bill, squeezing every budget category to reduce expenses, and being disciplined in sticking to our monthly Excel spreadsheet budget, we were able to pay off $4,500 in debt within a year! It has been hard and there are days that I deal with burnout, but now that we are earning interest instead of always paying it, we won't ever go back."

—Dawn D., wife and mom of three,
MoneySavingMom.com reader

Implementing a budget takes work, time, and serious commitment. You have to stick with it—even when it's hard. But it will be every bit worth it. A budget gives purpose to your money and it frees you up to enjoy living life rather than spending most of your time worrying about how you're going to afford to live. And that, my friends, is one of the most peaceful feelings in all the world!

CHAPTER FOUR

GO TOTALLY PLASTIC-FREE— TEMPORARILY

Now comes the tough part of budgeting, the part that maybe you secretly hoped you could avoid implementing. Look—you can budget to your heart's content, meticulously accounting for each penny or creating neat little cells in your spreadsheet. But if you never actually follow through with it—guess what? You're going to stay stuck in exactly the same position you're in right now. That's not good enough!

The best way to get motivated to get going on your budget is to cut out all the plastic you pay with completely for three months. That means your credit cards—*and* your debit cards.

RULE #4: TAKE THE CASH-ONLY CHALLENGE

What? Think it's crazy? Too time-consuming? Incompatible with your shop-online lifestyle? Here's the simple truth:

credit and debit cards give you a false sense of security and the opportunity to cheat on your budget when the temptation arises. Even if you have the best intentions, when you use a credit or debit card to manage your budget, there's always—even if it's only psychological—a cushion built in. You have something in place to fall back on *just this one time*, or, as is often the case with credit cards, *just until payday*.

No more. I've put together an easy, step-by-step plan for you to temporarily put down the plastic. This exercise will likely be very difficult—maybe even more difficult than getting your home organized or creating a budget. I promise I'm not suggesting this to make your life miserable, though. Quite the opposite. You see, I want you to experience the freedom that comes from living without consumer debt. I want you to be in charge of your money, telling it exactly where you want it to go and exactly what you want it to do. I want you to be able to live without worrying how you're going to pay for your basic necessities. I want you to be able to have money left over to put toward savings goals, to be able to give generously to needs in your community and around the world, and to be able to splurge occasionally on things you enjoy.

The best way to jump-start yourself toward financial success is to commit to buy only what you can afford. And if you don't already have the money set aside for it, you can't afford it. It's that simple. Swiping a card—whether debit or credit—makes it easy to buy things you can't afford. Even if you use only a debit card and have a strict budget, it's easier to go a little over your budget when you're swiping a card.

How We Spent $300 More a Month
Using Our Debit Card

We did an experiment a few years ago. Instead of using cash to pay for things like groceries, gas, going out to eat, and other shopping like we've always done, we switched to swiping our debit card almost exclusively.

Would you believe that we discovered that we spent, on average, around $300 more per month when swiping a debit card versus using cash? That adds up to be somewhere around $3,600 extra spent per year when we swiped a card instead of using cash. That could pay for a sturdy little used car. Or, in five years, it could be enough to put a good down payment on a house.

You might be shaking your head at this point, thinking, I'm glad that you found that you spend less when you use cash, but you're different than me. In fact, I'm positive that I will spend more money using cash than I spend with my credit or debit card.

I hear this a lot from my blog readers when I encourage them to consider going cold turkey and only use cash. But of all the people who have made this excuse, I've only known a handful of people who have actually tried a three-month Cash-Only Challenge and found this to be true. Most people who take the Cash-Only Challenge find that they actually *save* quite a bit of money by using cash.

Paying with cash can also give you a much better grasp on your finances and on where your money is going. You can no longer disassociate the pain of paying for something from the purchase. It's immediate: you take the cash out of the cash envelope, you make your purchase, and you then have fewer green bills in your envelope. This direct correlation can be felt clearly only when you pay with cash.

How Lois and Rick Paid Off Their Credit Card Debt and Student Loan By Using Cash

"For years, our family didn't have a budget. We used our debit card and, when things were really tight, we used our credit card. At the encouragement of a friend, my husband and I finally sat down and figured out a budget.

"We stopped using debit and credit cards completely and went to using only cash for everything. I calculated how much all of our monthly bills would cost, and we made these our first priority in the budget. Then we took everything that was left over and put it toward paying off our credit cards. Once we paid those off, we then started paying off my student loan.

"Within a year, sticking with a budget and using cash gave us enough extra money each month to pay off our credit cards and the student loan. We are now paying off our mortgage and using the extra money to fund our children's college accounts, save for a vacation and some furniture, as well as fund a Roth IRA for both my husband and myself.

"Using cash and sticking with a budget has completely changed the way we do things, and I love it. I don't stress anymore about the checkbook getting too low because we went on an unplanned spending spree. We still go on occasional spending sprees, but now we budget for them and only use the cash we've allotted for them."

TAKE THE CASH-ONLY CHALLENGE

1. Cut up, freeze, or otherwise completely remove your ability to use a credit or debit card for the next three months.

2. Make sure you've created a Full-fledged Budget as outlined in chapter 3. If not, do not try the Cash-Only Challenge. Instead, go back and follow the steps in chapter 3 to get on a written budget.

3. Determine which categories from your Full-fledged Budget will be paid from your cash envelopes and which categories will be paid by direct withdrawal or check. Use cash for as many categories as you possibly can. Only use a check or automatic withdrawal for those categories that are a fixed rate or that you are never tempted to overspend in. If you're paying bills online, choose the automatic withdrawal option that allows you to enter your checking account and bank routing numbers and then your payments will be automatically taken out of your account on a monthly basis. Note: *I do not recommend setting up automatic withdrawal on debt payments. Giving creditors unfettered access to your checking account can be dangerous as they may clean your account*

out to pay your debt. Instead, send a check or make a payment online that is authorized for a specific amount.

Calculate how much cash you need to withdraw on a monthly basis to fund each of your budget categories. If you get paid on a monthly basis, you'll not need to worry about this as you'll just divide up your paycheck according to what your specific budget categories are. But if you get paid every other week or weekly, you'll want to know exactly how much of each paycheck should be set aside for each category so that it adds up to the monthly budgeted amount for that category. We have these biweekly amounts written next to each category in our budget.

4. Divide up your paycheck as soon as you receive it: immediately deposit enough money in your checking account to cover all the monthly expenses paid by check or automatic withdrawal and withdraw cash in the total amount needed for your cash envelopes and divvy it up between the cash envelopes.

5. Bring only your cash envelope and a calculator with you when you shop. When I am buying groceries, I make a grocery list based upon what's on sale at the store and what I have on hand (more on how I do that in the next chapter). I do a quick estimate ahead of time on how much my shopping list should total. I bring this amount plus a little extra to the store. (For us, that's $5 to $10 extra.) You'll want to decide what works for you. But remember that when the cash envelope money is gone, it's gone. So use it wisely!

6. When shopping at the grocery store or another store where you're making multiple purchases, calculate your purchases on the calculator as you add them to your cart. This will motivate you to evaluate all purchases carefully, make you aware of how much items actually cost, encourage you to look for the best deal, and prevent you from getting up to the register and having to put something back because your total is higher than what you have in your cash envelope. (Been there, done that and, believe me, it's embarrassing!)

7. When making online purchases, use PayPal, a prepaid card, or a gift card. Some prepaid cards have fees attached to them, so I'd recommend paying through PayPal (linked directly to your bank account). Check the appropriate cash envelope that the purchase will be coming out of to make sure that you have enough money to cover it. If so, make the purchase through PayPal and deposit the money into the bank right away or else stick it in an envelope marked "To Deposit" which you can then deposit the next time you're headed to the bank. (You'll want to make sure you have enough in your account to cover the online purchase if you won't be depositing the cash right away.)

It might seem like a hassle to refund the money to your bank account when you make an online purchase, but not only does this guarantee that you stick with your budget, it also encourages you to be more thoughtful about what you spend. Instead of just jumping on a good deal—without even thinking—because you're afraid it might not be available for long, having to take the money out of your cash envelope and deposit it into your bank account forces you to think through whether it's a good deal for you and whether it's something you can really afford.

8. If you don't spend all the money in a budget category or cash envelope during a month, don't see that as license to go blow it on something else. Just save it and roll it over to the next month. It's good to have wiggle room, and you never know if there's a future expense in that category you'll need it for. Most of the time, such as with the auto repairs category, we eventually need to use most of it, even if it sits and accumulates without being touched for months. It's so reassuring to know that we have a budget category that is fully funded for auto repairs if the car breaks down or a tire blows.

"Having a certain amount in cash has really helped me develop the discipline of saying, Enough's enough."

—Jenny Whitney, MoneySavingMom.com reader

WHAT IF I FIND A GOOD DEAL BUT DON'T HAVE THE CASH ON HAND?

What if you see something that seems like a really great deal you can't pass up? Well, remember that little extra you put in your envelope before you went out shopping? Now you can evaluate if it's truly a good deal by determining if it's worth spending your extra money. Ask yourself, "Do I really need this?" "Is it in the budget?" If the answer is yes, it can go in the cart. If there's not enough extra cash to cover it but you know it's too good a deal to pass up, having cash forces you to make tough choices to stay on budget: you can skip buying something else on your list that you can do without in order to afford it. After weighing these options, you'll probably find yourself putting the too-good-to-pass-up steal back on the shelf more often than not.

WHAT ABOUT ALL THE COINS?

If you use cash for most of your purchases, you will inevitably end up with a lot of loose change. You can keep this in the designated cash envelope or you can drop these coins into a piggy bank and let them accumulate over the course of the year to use toward a fun family outing or something extra you are saving for.

SURELY YOU'RE NOT SAYING I SHOULD CUT UP MY DEBIT AND CREDIT CARDS FOR THE REST OF MY LIFE, ARE YOU?

We don't use credit cards. In fact, we don't own them—not even for "emergencies." Believe it or not, I've never even had a credit card! I know some of my nearest and dearest friends use them, and I've seen people use them while living beneath their means and meticulously sticking with their budget. However, I can say with great certainty that if you don't have *enormous* self-control, you shouldn't be using a credit card. You are only asking for financial trouble—and possibly even ruin.

My friend Trent, who blogs at TheSimpleDollar.com, gives this warning about credit cards: "Effective credit card use requires a lot of self-control. I am speaking from experience here—I learned the hard way about what damage a credit card can do if you don't have self-control. It took a mountain of debt and a point that was perilously close to personal bankruptcy (while having a baby at home, no less) to force me to wake up to the truth—that a credit card without self-control is like a chainsaw in the hands of a toddler."[4] I heartily agree. I've heard so many stories from Money SavingMom.com readers of the devastation credit cards can wreak in one's life if you're not incredibly careful.

"A credit card without self-control is like a chainsaw in the hands of a toddler."

—Trent Hamm, TheSimpleDollar.com

---

[4] http://www.thesimpledollar.com/2009/12/13/interest-rates-dont-matter-if-you-dont-carry-a-balance-some-thought-on-the-cash-only-debate/

WHY CREDIT CARDS CAN BE
YOUR WORST ENEMY

- **Credit cards can encourage you to spend money you don't have.** Credit cards offer the opportunity, like almost nothing else, for instant gratification. When you swipe, you don't have to think of the long-term consequences or worry whether there's money in your bank account.

- **Credit cards can encourage you to buy things you don't need.** The physical act of paying with cash makes an impression swiping a credit card never can. That physical connection to your cash makes you feel the pain of parting with it, and suddenly you start to notice how all your little extra expenses add up: that trip through the drive-through lane, that latte on the way to work, that candy bar at the gas station. While those careless little splurges might not seem like much—$2.50 here, $5 there, 99¢ over here—they add up quickly.

- **Credit cards make it easy to become a statistic.** Citing government debt data and census data, IndexCreditCards .com estimates the average household credit card debt at $9,858.[5] Chances are, you're not going to be the exception to the rule: credit card companies have vast resources at their disposal to make sure that you aren't.

- **Credit cards encourage you to bank on the future.** So many people say, "I treat my credit card like cash and always pay off my credit card bill in full at the end of each

[5] http://www.indexcreditcards.com/creditcarddebt/

month." Unless, before you make a purchase, you set aside the full amount of money to cover the purchase in a separate account and never touch that money until you pay your credit card bill, you are not truly treating your credit cards like cash.

If you don't have the money set aside for the full credit card bill, what happens if you lose your job tomorrow or you have a major financial crisis that puts you in a big bind? By using the bank's money or store credit to pay for your purchases, you are presuming that you are going to have enough money to pay the bill when it comes. And if you don't, you could end up getting hit with high interest payments on top of the money you owe.

* **Credit cards discourage self-discipline and steal the fulfillment of working hard and saving to pay cash for purchases.** Paying on credit instead of paying with cash can never give you the sense of fulfillment that comes from working, waiting, and saving up to pay your own hard-earned money for something.

CASHBACK REWARDS: ONE OF THE BIGGEST RIPOFFS EVER

I can't even begin to count how many times I've mentioned that we don't use credit cards and people immediately respond with, "Well, we save so much money by using credit cards. In fact, we earned a vacation to France for our family of four last year—just by using our credit cards!"

Did you ever stop to think why the credit card companies are giving out such nice rewards? Let me assure you it is not just because they have hearts overflowing with generosity. In almost every case, the credit card companies are the beneficiaries in these schemes because they usually earn back far more in interest than they ever give out! In addition, these cash-back rewards can encourage you to *spend more*. And we all know that it's not truly saving money if you spend more money in order to earn more credit card rewards.

WHAT ABOUT TRAVELING? WON'T I NEED TO USE A CREDIT CARD?

If you travel often, you will need to use a credit card or debit card to make online hotel or flight reservations or to rent a car. Unfortunately, cash or PayPal does not work in these instances.

If there's no other option besides paying with debit or credit, I always choose to pay with a debit card. I don't have a credit card, for starters. But more important, I don't want to bank on the future by paying for something with someone else's money.

There is a bit more of a risk in using a debit card online versus a credit card. For instance, if someone has fraudulently used your credit card, you aren't saddled with the charges, but if someone has fraudulently used your debit card, the money comes directly out of your account. You'll have to wait for your bank to do an examination of their records to investigate your fraud claim.

One of the reasons that my husband and I believe

strongly in having an emergency fund of at least three to six months' of expenses in the bank is to have a fallback in case something like this happens. However, while people tend to cite the fact that you could temporarily be out thousands of dollars as one of the major reasons not to use debit cards, we had a few thousand dollars fraudulently charged to our debit card once and with a few phone calls, the bank reversed the charges.

So it doesn't have to be as awful as many people make it out to be. In addition, most people don't realize that most debit cards offer the exact same amount of protection as credit cards do. (And if your debit card doesn't have built-in fraud protection, it's high time you switch to a different card.)

If you discover an unauthorized transfer on your account, your loss is limited to $50 provided you notify your financial institution within two business days. If you do not report the fraudulent charges within two days, you could be out as much as $500. If you wait more than 60 days to report the fraudulent charges, you could risk unlimited loss, meaning you could potentially lose all the money in your account.

HOW TO PROTECT YOURSELF
FROM ONLINE FRAUD

1. Watch Your Accounts Like a Hawk

It is your responsibility to check your accounts to make sure no one is using them fraudulently. Log in to your accounts at least once every day or every other day to make sure all charges showing up are correct. In the event that something is incorrect, deal with it immediately to prevent a lot of hassle later.

2. Don't Buy from Sites That Aren't Secure

If you're going to fill in your debit card information on any site, make sure that the website address begins with https://. If it doesn't, do not complete the order as the site is not secure and a scammer could easily farm your credit card information. Also, make sure that there is a lock icon showing somewhere at the top of your browser.

3. Don't Give Out Information Unless You're Sure a Site Is Legitimate

If you have doubts about the legitimacy of a site or just want to double check, first make sure that the checkout area of the site is secure. Second, look for any glaring errors, multiple misspellings, or a site that just looks hastily put together. Finally, you can type in the website address at Domains.Whois.com and it will tell you who owns the site, the address of the owner, and when the domain name (site address) was set up. If a site was set up in the last six months or if the site appears to be U.S.-based, but the site address owner is from another country, be very leery of it.

4. Check Your Credit Report Twice a Year

Check your credit report once every six months. You can get a free copy of your credit report up to three times per year (once per year per credit reporting agency) from AnnualCredit Report.com. Checking your credit report does not negatively affect your credit score in any way.

BUT WHAT ABOUT MY CREDIT SCORE?!?

We're a culture obsessed with credit scores. I bet some of you are saying, "This is all fine and good, Crystal, but what about my credit score? I can't survive in this day and age without it!" What we often forget is what a credit score is really about: the ability to amass more debt. Your credit score is calculated entirely based upon your past and present debt and how faithful (or unfaithful) you've been in keeping up with your payments. The more late and outstanding payments you have, the lower your score. The better your track record in paying your debts on time, the higher your score.[6]

The bizarre thing, though, is that people like me who have never had a credit card in their life, have always paid their bills on time, have money in the bank, have no debt, and have a steady income, have *zero* credit. While this might seem like a good thing, it has actually made life a little difficult: we had to have someone cosign on our first apartment lease, and I couldn't set up my cell phone plan without putting down a $500 deposit. My husband did have a credit card for a year in order to build up credit, so he's been able to have things in his name, which has helped. However, I understand that it is wise to have credit—especially if you are just starting out and need to get an apartment or set up a phone plan and don't have the extra cash in your budget to put down a sizable deposit.

If you are out of debt, on a good budget, and have successfully shown discipline in handling your money for at least two or three years, I'm going to outline a simple way to

---

[6] http://www.myfico.com/crediteducation/whatsinyourscore.aspx

build your credit without getting burned. **Do not focus on building your credit if you are not on a solid budget and living on less than you make or if you have any outstanding debt aside from school loans or a mortgage on your home.** Throwing your energies into implementing a workable game plan for where your money goes every month is going to be much more effective for your finances in the long run than a good credit score will be. *Never* use a credit card unless you have tremendous self-control and discipline. If you don't have a complete commitment to stick fastidiously to your budget and not be deterred no matter how tempted you might be, stay as far away from credit cards as possible.

HOW TO BUILD YOUR CREDIT WITHOUT GETTING BURNED

1. **Get a credit card with a $500 limit.** Don't put it in your wallet; put it in your safe instead. If it's out of easy reach, you won't be tempted to use it for an unexpected expense. Budget for these "unexpected expenses" as much as possible and have an Emergency Fund so that you have some cushion to pay cash when something breaks, the car dies, or you have unforeseen medical expenses. Do not ever use this credit card for an emergency!

2. **Set up payments for one of your utility bills (or another must-pay monthly bill) to be paid directly from this credit card.** Pick a "boring" bill that doesn't fluctuate much over the course of a year and one on which you

won't be tempted to overspend (i.e., do not choose to pay for entertainment or your clothes budget category as a way to build your credit).

3. **Plan ahead and always have enough money in your utility bill budget category** to cover your credit card bill before it comes due.

   Continue with this system for at least a year or two until you have a good credit score established. Once your healthy credit is established, cut up the credit card, and never look back.

CHAPTER FIVE

COUPONS ARE NOT JUST FOR JUNK FOOD

In the first four chapters, we've talked about a lot of foundational principles—things that can completely revamp the way you handle your finances. Goal setting, budgeting, and overhauling your financial game plan are not necessarily fun, but they are vitally necessary for financial success. Once you get those things in place, you're ready to jump into the fun stuff. Namely, finding creative ways to shave hundreds—or even thousands!—of dollars off your existing budget.

If you're looking to lower your expenditures, I always encourage people to start with their grocery budget because it's one of the easiest and most pain-free places to start. Plus, everyone has to buy groceries, so you might as well save a bundle while doing something you already must do! Yes, it will take some effort, and, no, you likely won't see 75 percent in grocery savings overnight, but I can guarantee that if you implement the principles I outline in the following two chapters, in the next few months you'll reduce your grocery bill by at least 30 percent to 50 percent—or even more! If you typically spend $200 per week on groceries and household items for a family of five, that's a savings of $60 to $100 per week—for just an hour or two of extra work. That's like making $30 to $50 dollars per hour. Best of all, this savings is tax-free!

RULE #5: USE COUPONS

I believe everyone should use coupons. There. I said it. Wait. I take my statement back. If you are one of the .0002 people in America who has never touched food unless it was grown in your own yard, you make toothpaste out of tree bark, and use cloth toilet paper, then I'll exempt you.[7] But the rest of you? You're nonexempt.

YES, THERE ARE LOTS OF COUPONS FOR ORGANIC AND NATURAL PRODUCTS

Contrary to what many people think, coupons are not just for junk and processed food. If you look through the coupon inserts in the Sunday newspaper, you're going to see many coupons for processed foods. And it can be discouraging if you're trying to save money while still eating natural, healthful foods.

---

[7] I made up the .0002 statistic, since I couldn't find any actual studies on this and I don't think it's possible to make toothpaste out of tree bark, but people seriously do use cloth toilet paper. I'm not making that up! Just Google it. Or, um, maybe don't. I might be frugal, but I'm not anywhere near *that* frugal!

But the truth is, if you know where to look (more on that a little later!), you'll find there are often coupons available for baking supplies, cheese, milk, eggs, lightbulbs, batteries, toilet paper, toothbrushes, razors, sponges, and many other items that aren't normally labeled "junk food" or aren't even food to begin with. There are also many coupons available for organic foods, fresh fruit and vegetables, and even meat.

IF YOU USE COUPONS CORRECTLY, YOU'LL SAVE AT LEAST $25 TO $50 PER HOUR

If you buy the Sunday paper, clip all the coupons, and then use them all on your next shopping trip, you're probably not going to save any money. Instead, you'll likely end up buying a lot of overpriced items you won't use or wouldn't normally buy and spending a considerable amount more than you save. That's not how to use coupons. Using coupons wisely requires strategy and patience. In most cases, it involves waiting until an item is at its rock-bottom price and then pairing it with a coupon so that you get it for pennies on the dollar—or even more than free! If you take the time to learn how to use coupons correctly and are willing to put forth at least one hour's worth of work each week, you can save at least $25 to $50 for every hour you invest in strategic shopping.

"I am a single mom with four children. I also have severe back issues that leave me unable to work full-time. Thanks to couponing, I am able to purchase brand-name items at a fraction of the retail price and I am able to make sure my college-age children have the items they need like razors, shampoo, and laundry detergent. I am also able to donate to our local food banks or help out needy families—something that makes me feel good especially on my limited income."

—Heather, MoneySavingMom.com reader

READY, SET, START COLLECTING!

One of the most-often-asked questions I receive when people see my shopping trips and see that I'll buy multiples of the same item and use more than one of the same coupon is, "How do you get so many coupons?" As most people know, there are coupon inserts in your local Sunday newspaper. That's a great place to start, especially if you already have a newspaper subscription. If you don't have a newspaper subscription, you can usually get the best deal on newspapers through DiscountedNewspapers.com. I suggest trying to pay no more than $2 per week if you are purchasing the newspaper only for coupons.

There are four different companies that include coupon inserts in the Sunday paper: SmartSource, RedPlum, General Mills, and P&G. It varies each week what inserts are included, but there are usually one to three different inserts. On major holiday weekends (such as Christmas), there are usually no inserts. You can see the schedule of what inserts will be in upcoming Sunday newspapers at http://www.taylortownpreview.com/index.htm.

Tip: As coupons are often released as market research for food corporations, different areas of the country often get different coupons and coupon values. Bigger cities tend to get more coupons and higher-value coupons ($1 off as opposed to only 50¢), so if you don't live in a big city, I recommend calling around to newspaper publishers in cities that are within one to two hours of your home to see if they offer discounts for out-of-town subscribers.

NINE WAYS TO GET COUPONS FOR FREE

1. Ask friends, relatives, and coworkers for their extra coupon inserts. Start asking around and see if anyone you know already gets the Sunday paper and doesn't use the coupons from it. You might be surprised at how many coupon inserts just get thrown out. You could offer to share a few of your free-after-coupon products each month in exchange for someone saving their newspaper inserts for you. MoneySavingMom.com reader, Jessica, says: "I asked coworkers and friends to save their coupon inserts for me, rather than purchasing or subscribing to the Sunday paper. About every three months, I bake a batch of brownies or cookies to thank my pals for their kindness!"

Tip: Looking for more coupons? Consider asking on your local Freecycle.org or Craigslist.com if anyone in your area has extra coupon inserts. Alissia says, "I posted on both of these sites and was able to find people in my area who don't use the coupons out of their papers. I now pick up a huge stack of coupons every couple of weeks from them."

2. Stop by Starbucks or McDonald's on Sunday afternoons. Many people purchase Sunday papers, read them at Starbucks, McDonald's, and other similar venues, and then leave them. A few friends of mine stop by area Starbucks and/or McDonald's locations on Sunday afternoons and are usually able to pick up at least three to five complete coupon inserts from extra newspapers left behind by customers at each location. Know someone who works at restaurants like this? They might be able to collect the leftover coupon inserts and give them to you later in the week. In addition, some gas stations will also give you their extra unsold Sunday newspapers on Sunday evening or Monday morning. It never hurts to ask.

3. Make friends with someone who delivers newspapers. Not all areas allow this, but some people who deliver Sunday newspapers are able to pass on any leftover newspapers and coupon inserts to other people. Or you might be able to find the recycling center they drop them off at and obtain them there. As always, make sure

that this is legal in your area. You do not want to be getting fined for stealing or to put someone's job in jeopardy over getting some free coupons!

4. Trade coupons. Trading coupons is a great way to get coupons you need in exchange for giving away coupons you don't need. For instance, if you have a dog and don't have children in diapers, and I have children in diapers and don't have a dog, we could trade diaper and dog food coupons. You can trade coupons with people in your own area or you can join coupon-trading forums online and trade with people from all over the country. While it will cost you postage, it may be worth it to trade coupons with others online—especially if you're able to pick and choose specific coupons you'd like. Also remember that different regions of the country get different coupons. Trading with people from other states allows you to diversify your coupon portfolio and collect high-value coupons you wouldn't have access to in your local paper.

Tip: HotCouponWorld.com/forums/ has some very active coupon trading forums. I've never used them myself, but they have come highly recommended.

5. Join Coupon Trains. Allen Williams shared a great explanation of a coupon train in his article on Suite 101: "Before the internet, people wanting to save money with coupons

would turn to joining or forming a coupon train. A train is maintained by one person who sends an envelope of coupons through postal mail. The package contains a mailing list, and as one person takes and adds coupons to the envelope, it is mailed to the next coupon train recipient on the mailing list. Coupon trains allow individuals between cities, or even across states and provinces, to organize and share coupons. By establishing a group, the coupon train leverages each person's coupon clipping power to share coupons with a larger audience."[8]

Interested in joining a Coupon Train? I'd suggest starting at: http://www.HotCouponWorld.com/forums/coupon-trains-hop-board/.

6. Check your local public library. Most public libraries receive newspaper subscriptions. Often, they will allow you to have the coupon inserts from their Sunday papers if you just ask.

7. Pick up coupons at the store. Keep your eyes peeled at the store and pick up any coupons you find on tearpads or in the blinking dispensers. If there are plenty of extras, snag multiple copies of these. A lot of times, this very item will be on an exceptional sale just a few weeks later and you'll be more than glad you picked up that handful of coupons!

8. Write and ask for coupons. What products do you regularly use and love but rarely find good coupons for?

---

[8] http://www.suite101.com/content/how-to-save-on-groceries-with-a-coupon-train-a145120

Write to the manufacturer, tell them how much you like their product, and politely request that they send you any coupons they have available (don't forget to include your mailing address, too!). Usually, it takes only a few minutes to do so through a company's contact form on their website, and you'll very likely get some sort of coupons just for asking. In many cases, you'll receive high-value coupons or even free product coupons!

Tip: Many companies offer high-value coupons or coupons for free items in exchange for your willingness to become their fan on Facebook or sign up for their email newsletter. I suggest setting up a separate free email account through Gmail.com to use when signing up for free items or coupons. Check out Freebies4Mom.com for daily updates on the best freebies offered around the web. Even if you're not a mom, you'll find lots of great stuff to sign up for!

9. Print coupons online. If your grocery stores accept printable coupons, the internet can be an almost limitless source of printable coupons. Best of all, many times the coupons available to print online are much higher than what you'll find in the newspaper inserts.

    Some of the best sources for printable coupons are: Coupons.com, SmartSource.com, RedPlum.com, Mambo Sprouts.com (organic printable coupons), and Printable CouponsandDeals.com. In addition, you can check out the coupon database on my site: http://MoneySaving Mom.com/print-coupons/coupon-database, which allows you to search for any product or item by name and it will pull up all printable (and newspaper insert) coupons available for that product.

Tip: To save money, use both sides of paper when printing coupons, change the settings on your printer to Grayscale (this will only use black ink) and print in Fast Draft Mode (this uses less ink).

GET THEM FILED: THE THREE BEST COUPON ORGANIZATIONAL METHODS

Once you start accumulating a nice stash of coupons, you'll quickly need to come up with an organizational system because the coupons will do you no good if they are a complete, disorganized mess! There are a number of different ways to organize your coupons and there is no one "right" way. When you're first starting out, don't feel like you have to go get yourself some massive box or binder in order to use coupons correctly. It's perfectly okay to start with a little index box or something like the organizational system offered from TheCouponizer.com. The goal is to save money with coupons, not to create some elaborate system. Don't get hung up on all the details. Keep it simple—especially at first.

If you feel like you're outgrowing a system or it's just not working well for you, I encourage you to experiment with a few different organizational methods to determine what works best for you.

The Coupon Box Method

The Coupon Box organizational method consists of a rectangular plastic clasping bin with a lid and individual categorical envelopes. You can use letter-size envelopes or small letter envelopes (No. 6¾ – 3⅝ x 6½ in,) and just cut the flaps off and staple an index card with a category written on it standing up inside. The envelopes are organized alphabetically with the main categories and then multiple envelopes for each main category. Mine are color-coded for easier retrieval in the store.

Here are all the categories I have in my Coupon Box (the items in parentheses are each of the separate envelopes):

Baby (diapers, products, wipes)

Bags (containers, foil/plastic wrap)

Baking (mixes, oil/sugar)

Batteries

Beverages

Bread

Candy

Canned (meat, soup, vegetables, fruit)

Cereal (envelopes for each brand)

Cleaner (all-purpose, bathroom, dish detergent, disinfectant, laundry, furniture polish, floor, glass)

Condiments

Crackers

Dairy (beverage, cheese, sour cream/cream cheese/butter, snacks, yogurt)

Frozen (beverage, bread, ice cream, meat, snacks, vegetables/fruit/potatoes)

Health Food

Hygiene (Band-Aids, deodorant, face, feminine, hair, lotion, medicine/vitamins, shaving, soap)

Jelly, Peanut Butter

Meat

Mexican

Office Supplies

Paper Products (facial tissue, cups/plates, toilet tissue, towels/napkins)

Pasta

Rice

Salad Dressing

Sauce

Seasonings

Snacks

Syrup

Toothbrushes

Toothpaste

Pros: Since I've used this method for more than ten years, I happen to be partial to it. I love that you have every coupon at your fingertips. Plus, filing coupons is a breeze because you just drop them into the appropriate envelope instead of having to fold and stuff them like you do in the baseball sleeves of a Coupon Binder (discussed below).

Cons: The box is a little bulky and might feel conspicuous to some of you to take into a store. In addition, if you drop the box, you may have Coupon Disorganization Disaster! You can't see every coupon you have as easily without shuffling through the category envelope, unlike the Coupon Binder where you can flip open a page and see all the coupons at a glance. And finally, you have to keep up with cutting and filing coupons.

The Binder Method

This method of coupon organization is probably the most popular. There are many different ways to create a coupon binder, but they all usually involve categorizing coupons in a three-ring zippered binder with the coupons filed in plastic baseball card holder sleeves. You can create your own system or purchase one premade. I'd suggest creating it yourself unless you are absolutely sure it's worth the expense of buying a premade one.

Pros: You can easily see all your coupons at a glance, making it simple to locate coupons. Unlike the Coupon Box method, if you drop the Coupon Binder, you don't have to worry about coupons scattering everywhere!

Cons: When I tried this method, I found it tedious to put all the coupons in the sleeves. If they didn't fit, you'd have to fold them and stuff them in. It took quite a bit of time and effort compared to my Coupon Box method.

The Whole Insert Method

This method of coupon organization is the least time consuming. Instead of clipping out coupons, you keep the inserts from the Sunday newspapers whole and file them by date in file folders in a filing box. When you are planning your shopping trips, you'll look for the date of the insert that a particular coupon you want to use is in and then you can just pull that insert out of your file box and clip the coupon you want to use.

Tip: As I mentioned earlier, I have a searchable coupon database on MoneySavingMom.com that allows you to search for a product or brand and then bring up all the matching coupons by date and insert. For instance, if you're looking for a coupon for Bird's Eye vegetables because they are on sale at your store for just $1 per

bag this week, you can search "Bird's Eye" and it will pull up all printable and insert coupons for Bird's Eye products. The list of results will include the direct link(s) to print the coupon(s) or the date(s) and name(s) of the Sunday newspaper(s) the coupon(s) were in. In addition, it will tell you the value of the coupon ($1 off, etc.) and when the coupon expires. Using a coupon database can save you a great deal of time as well as help you find coupons you might not otherwise remember about or dig up.

....

Pros: *The Whole Insert Method is simple and perfect for a person who doesn't have a lot of time to clip coupons. In addition, it's easy to find your coupons when you're planning your grocery shopping trip by searching for a coupon on the coupon database and then just pulling the insert from the file and clipping the coupon.*

Cons: *Since you don't clip all your coupons with this method, if you run into a great clearance or un-advertised deal at the store, you won't be able to search your coupons to see if you have any you could use. This was the most frustrating aspect when I tried this method. I missed out on deal after deal because I didn't have my whole Coupon Box at my fingertips. In addition, you can't check to see all the coupons you have for a specific product or category at a glance.*

These are the three basic methods used by couponers. Experiment and figure out what works for you, or do a search online for "coupon organizational methods" to pull up a host of variations to these methods that others have detailed on their blogs and websites.

Tip: Don't throw out your expired coupons. Instead, mail them to people in the military who are stationed overseas, since they can use them at the commissary for up to six months after the expiration date. To find details on which military bases are accepting coupons and where to send them, visit http://ocpnet.org.

CHAPTER SIX

BEYOND THE BASICS: ADVANCED COUPONING TECHNIQUES

Now that I've taught you where to find coupons and how to organize them, it's time to kick things up a notch and learn how to save really big by combining coupons with sales. Remember to take it slow and don't try to learn everything at once. Even just steadily lowering your grocery by 2 percent to 3 percent each month is progress! And over time, that can add up to very significant savings! In fact, if you consistently lowered your grocery bill by 2 percent to 3 percent every month for a year, by the end of the year, you'd be paying around 30 percent less for groceries!

SHOP AT MORE THAN ONE STORE TO KEEP YOUR BUDGET DOWN

When I mention how I save a lot of money by shopping at more than one store, I'm often met with resistance: "But I don't have time to go to more than one store! I can barely make it into Walmart once a week." "That's not saving money! You're wasting all sorts of time and gas running around to fifteen different stores in one day. Wouldn't it be more cost effective and efficient to just do all your shopping at one store each week?"

Yes, one can make a lot of excuses for not shopping at more than one store. But I think all of these excuses show a lack of understanding about what it really means to shop at more than one store. Let me be clear: I am not advocating going to fifteen different stores that are forty-five minutes away from your home in order to save $2 at each store. That's not saving money, in my definition. Instead, that's wasting enormous amounts of time and effort and producing little to show for it but wear and tear on your vehicle and an exorbitant gas bill. What I am advocating is taking a little bit of time to scout at your nearby stores each week and pick a few that have the best sales and deals. Then base your grocery trip planning on shopping only at those stores.

HOW TO SHOP AT MORE THAN ONE STORE WITHOUT SPENDING HOURS EACH WEEK SHOPPING

Consider your options. Shopping for groceries doesn't only have to happen at stores that are specifically designed as "grocery stores." Consider all the options in your area that sell food and household items:

- Co-ops
- Dollar stores

- Scratch-and-dent stores
- Overstock stores (Big Lots, etc.)
- Big box stores (KMart, Walmart, Target)
- Warehouse stores (Costco, Sam's Club, B.J.'s)
- Drugstores (CVS, Walgreens, Rite Aid)
- Asian markets
- Bulk food stores
- Community-supported agriculture groups (check to see if there's one in your area at LocalHarvest.org)
- Farmers' markets
- Health food stores

Search online or pull out the phone book to see what non-grocery store options you have in your area. Ask your friends and neighbors if they know of any great places to shop that you might not know about. If you live in a small town, this should be simple. In fact, you might have only one or two stores to choose from. If you live in a larger town or big metropolis, this is going to be a bigger undertaking. If you're feeling overwhelmed by all the options, limit the stores to those that are within a five-mile radius or are close to areas you regularly frequent.

Make a price book. A price book is basically just a notebook where you write down and track all the prices for items you regularly buy. If you're trying to decide which stores in your area typically have the best prices, I recommend going to at least a few of them and writing down the price of twenty-five items you routinely buy. Comparing the prices of twenty-five items at two to four different stores can help you determine which stores have lower everyday prices.

Tip: There's a price book form at the back of the book for you to copy and use. Or you can download free price book forms at MoneySavingMom.com.

Find out what your local store's coupon and markdown policies are. Your local store's coupon and markdown policies can make a big difference in the kind of deals you're able to get with coupons. Here are some things you'll want to know:

- Does this store double coupons? If so, up to what amount? Are there limitations on the doubling (some stores will double only one or three of the same kind of coupon per transaction).
- Does the store accept expired coupons?
- Does the store accept competitors' coupons?
- Does the store mark down produce, dairy, and meat on a regular basis? If so, what days and times does this usually occur?

Determine which store(s) in your area regularly have the lowest prices and best sales. After filling out the price book forms and finding out your local stores' coupon policies and markdown policies, you will have a pretty clear picture of which stores are best to shop at on a regular basis. However, most stores run their sales cycles every twelve weeks or so, with a few incredible seasonal sales and special offers thrown in on occasion. To get a more accurate picture, I'd recommend tracking the sales at a few stores for three months. This does not mean that you need to go to five different stores and fill out a price book form every week. But I would recommend scanning the sales fliers at each store and actually visiting each store at least once a month.

Tip: Check http://MoneySavingMom.com/store_deals/ to find the best weekly deals at more than one hundred grocery stores around the country. You can also do an internet search for your store's name + "coupon match-ups" or "weekly deals" to find a blogger who is covering the deals at your local grocery store(s). This will save you a lot of time, effort, and legwork!

Shop at different stores each week. Ideally, you'll save the most if you shop at two to three stores on a weekly basis and purchase only those items that are on exceptional sales plus produce and milk. This might seem time-consuming and overwhelming, especially if you're used to only shopping at one store each week. It really doesn't have to take that much extra time, though, and you don't need to shop at five or eight stores every week in order to see incredible savings. In fact, I rarely shop at more than three stores in a week. I usually stop at either Aldi and/or Dillon's (a Kroger affiliate) and then shop at either the health food store (to look for markdowns), Walmart, Target, or Dollar Tree.

I don't think I've ever gone to all six stores in one week, and I rarely spend more than two hours total grocery shopping in any given week. When planning my menu and grocery list, I just briefly glance through the ads and coupon match-ups online for all six stores and also take into consideration my schedule for the week and what other errands I need to run (I often will combine a quick shopping trip with another errand in order to save fuel and time) and then decide which store(s) I'll shop at that week. So a typical month of shopping may look something like this:

- Week 1: Aldi, health food store, Target
- Week 2: Dillon's, Walmart
- Week 3: Aldi, health food store
- Week 4: Dillon's, Dollar Tree

By rotating what stores I shop at each week, I'm able to take advantage of deals that are available only at that particular store and stock up on enough to last us until I head back to that store again. For instance, our Dollar Tree carries Nature's Own bread, hamburger buns, hot dog buns, and Cinnamon Swirl Bread for just $1 per loaf. This is the best price available on high-quality sandwich bread and buns in our area, so I stop at least once each month and buy enough to last us for the next four weeks. I stick the bread in the freezer, and we use it as needed.

If the thought of shopping at more than one store each week is overwhelming to you, never fear! Just start by picking two stores that consistently have the best deals and then rotate shopping at one of them per week based upon which has the best weekly deals.

*Tip: If you live in a rural area where you have very
limited options, it probably won't be feasible for you to
shop at multiple stores on a regular basis. However, you
could consider making a trip to a larger city once every
month or two to stock up on items that are much less
expensive than your small town grocery store prices.
You'd want to do the math and make sure you were
actually saving a good chunk of money when factoring
in the gas and time to drive to a neighboring large town
with multiple grocery stores.*

PLAY THE DRUGSTORE GAME

One day in 2005, I had some extra time on my hands, so I
was researching new ideas for ways to save money. At the
time, my husband was in law school, we had one child, we
were living in a little basement apartment, and money was
extremely tight. So we were always looking for new ways
to pinch pennies even harder or make a little extra income.
In my online searching that day, I landed upon a forum of
people discussing this store called CVS. As I read more on
this forum about people getting hundreds of dollars' worth
of products for free, I became very intrigued.

I'd never heard of CVS, but I was thrilled to discover
that a nearby drugstore was in the process of being con-
verted to one. I read and researched everything I could
find about shopping at CVS (which wasn't a lot back then,

since there weren't any blogs that had it all mapped out for you!) and then timidly walked into this drugstore and tried my hand at a simple transaction. To my surprise, the deal worked! I paid a few dollars out of pocket and got those same dollars plus a few more back in Extra Care Bucks (a receipt that prints at the register which you can use like cash on your next transaction). I practically floated out of that store like I'd just struck gold.

I went home, did more research, clipped some more coupons, mapped out another deal scenario, and went back the next day. Once again, the deal was successful—and I used the Extra Care Bucks I'd earned on my transaction the day before to pay for this deal. So this time, I spent less than $1 out of pocket and, after my coupons and Extra Care Bucks, I got back around $8! I was hooked.

It so happened that the month I discovered CVS was the October when CVS was pushing their Extra Care program really hard. And during that month they had no limits on the Extra Care deals. Meaning, for every tube of Colgate Max Fresh toothpaste you purchased at $2.99, you'd get $2.99 back in Extra Care Bucks (ECBs). Whether you bought two or twenty, you'd get $2.99 back for each and every one you purchased. Best of all, there were 75¢ off Colgate toothpaste coupons available online and in the newspapers. So, I'd make over 50¢ back in Extra Care Bucks for every toothpaste I purchased after the coupons, ECBs, and tax. And I'd use the ECBs earned from the last transaction to pay for my next transaction, so I'd often spend less than 30¢ out of pocket and get back even more ECBs than I had used!

Since we just had one child, the CVS store was close to

our house, my husband was in school and working, and we had practically no money, I went a little overboard on the CVS deals. In fact, in about three weeks, we'd gotten around $800 worth of groceries, household products, and health and beauty products—and spent less than $20 out of pocket! Plus, I had around $120 in Extra Care Bucks waiting to be used. It was a bit insane!

Yes, I spent too much time at CVS and bought way too much toothpaste and other items that were free those first few weeks. I slowly learned to pace myself and eventually worked down to one or two shopping trips to CVS every week or every other week. I was still able to buy plenty of free and more-than-free deodorant, toothpaste, toothbrushes, shampoo, makeup, shaving cream, tissues, toilet paper, diapers, wipes, body wash, soap, medicine, and many other miscellaneous items to supply our little family, with plenty left over to share with others. This freed up a good percentage of our grocery budget! Plus, it was fun to try new products, many with a much higher retail tag than we'd ever usually pay.

The deals aren't quite as amazing as they were when I first started playing the "Drugstore Game" (as we couponers fondly refer to it!), but if you're willing to put forth thirty minutes of planning and thirty minutes of shopping at at least one drugstore every week, you can stock up on almost all the household, health, and beauty products your family needs for very little out of pocket. Think about it: if you got all of your toothpaste, razors, deodorant, shampoo, body wash, over-the-counter medicines, and all the other health and beauty products you routinely buy for free or almost free, wouldn't that significantly lower your grocery budget?

HOW TO GET STARTED PLAYING THE DRUGSTORE GAME

Pick one store to start with. If you have more than one drugstore chain in your area, please do yourself a huge favor and don't try to learn the ins and outs of CVS, Walgreens, and Rite Aid all at once. Start with one drugstore chain and learn the ropes of it before adding in another. I'd suggest beginning with CVS as it requires the least outlay of cash. You'll likely make some mistakes in the beginning, so the less cash you spend out of pocket, the better.

Read, read, read. Before you jump in with both feet, it's highly important that you take time to read up on how the drugstore rewards programs work and what their coupon policies are. It is vital to be well informed and well versed. Plus, it greatly increases your confidence level—and you need confidence in order to work the drugstore deals successfully. There are thousands of bloggers who cover the weekly deals at CVS, Rite Aid, and Walgreens. They'll show you pictures of their shopping trips, offer price breakdowns, and give you insider tips and unadvertised deal information. You can find links to step-by-step tutorials on how to shop at CVS, Walgreens, and Rite Aid at http://www.Money SavingMom.com/drugstores. You'll also find the best deals and coupon match-ups for the weekly deals at Walgreens, CVS, and Rite Aid posted at MoneySavingMom.com.

Start small. I know that it's easy to want to have some incredible transactions right out of the shoot where you get $80 worth of items for 22¢, but don't even think about going there yet. Start with a handful of items and work your way up. I'd suggest you plan your first drugstore shopping trip to be around $10 to $15 total. This is enough that you can learn the ropes, but not too much that you're out a bunch of money if you have some failed transactions.

Don't expect to do it perfectly. Notice I keep mentioning making mistakes? That's because pretty much everyone makes them when they are first learning. Even once you've armed yourself with lots of information and have reviewed deals incessantly before planning your own, you will very likely make some mistakes. It's okay. If you've never ridden a bike before, you usually don't just jump on and ride it flawlessly from the beginning. It takes practice and patience. The same is true with the Drugstore Game: you'll probably not have flawless transactions from the very get-go. But practice and patience will pay off in big dividends. So accept the mistakes you make as part of the learning process.

Be prepared with a backup plan. Oftentimes, drugstores will be out of an item that's part of the rewards offer or they won't even stock it. A backup plan is key. Work out two or three different scenario ideas and then make your final game plan once you're in the store and able to see what they have on hand. Also, find out when your local store restocks its shelves and plan your shopping trip somewhere near those times. It's frustrating to go in and find that they are completely out of everything that is free after rewards that week. You have a better chance of finding everything on your list if you shop right after they restock the shelves. In addition, if you don't see something in stock, be sure to ask if they might have extras in the back which they've not put on the shelves yet.

Tip: If your store is out of something, ask for a rain check. Most stores will willingly give these out and it can mean that while you didn't get to take advantage of the deal when you'd planned, you'll get to take advantage of it once the store restocks.

Commit to sticking with it for three months. While the Drugstore Game can save you a tremendous amount of money on household and beauty products, it's certainly not for everyone. You might find it takes more time and effort than it is worth for your family. For instance, since we've moved away from an area with a number of CVS stores and we don't have Rite Aid, I go to Walgreens only on occasion. While I miss the great deals at CVS, I'm able to keep our grocery budget low by using coupons at other stores in our area and following many other money-saving principles.

However, if you try your hand at the Drugstore Game and immediately find yourself frustrated, don't give up just yet. If you want to really see if it's worth it, commit to sticking with it for three months. Do at least one transaction every two weeks for three months and then evaluate at the end of the trial period whether you feel like this money-saving idea is worth the return on investment for you.

IMPLEMENT THE BUY-AHEAD PRINCIPLE

One of my biggest secrets for grocery saving success is that I practice the Buy-Ahead Principle. This means that other than dairy products and produce, I aim to never pay full price for anything. If you're willing to be patient and observant, you can buy most items at 50 percent or more off retail. When an item is 50 percent to 100 percent off its retail price, buy as many as you can afford in your grocery budget.

For example, say your family uses 10 tubes of toothpaste in a year's time and the retail price of toothpaste is $2.49. If you bought it at retail, you'd be paying $24.90 per year for toothpaste. If, however, you practiced the Buy-Ahead Principle, and you collected your $1 off toothpaste coupons and waited until toothpaste went on sale for $1 (which it does a few times per year in our area), you could buy 10 tubes of toothpaste for free. That's a savings of $24.90 per year! And that's just on toothpaste!

Here's another example of how this works. Target recently ran a frozen food deal where you got a $5 Target gift card for every seven frozen food items you purchased. Target frozen vegetables were $1.04 per bag and Target had printable coupons on its website for $1 off four bags. So I ended up buying more than 20 bags of frozen vegetables. I split my shopping trips up and used the $5 gift cards I earned from one trip to pay for the next trip. And I earned more gift cards on that trip. All in all, I got the vegetables for pennies per bag—a significant savings off the 89¢ to 99¢ price I usually pay at Aldi or my Kroger affiliate when they are already on a great sale. We won't eat 20 bags of frozen vegetables in a week, but we sure will eat 20 bags of frozen vegetables over the next two months! So I practiced the Buy-Ahead Principle, stocked up on frozen vegetables when they were at their rock-bottom price, and saved over $18 off the retail price. If you start implementing this principle when it comes to dozens of the groceries and household products you routinely buy, it begins to make a huge dent in your grocery bill.

How to Implement the Buy-Ahead Principle

- *Set Aside a Small Portion of Your Grocery Budget to Buying Ahead.* If this is a new concept for you, don't go out and spend $500 tomorrow on "good deals." You want to slowly apply the Buy-Ahead Principle so that you learn what you need, how much you use, and what is a rock-bottom price for your area. Set aside a percentage of your grocery budget each week (no more than 5 percent to 10 percent) to buying extra of those heavily discounted items that you know you will use sometime in the next few months.

- *Designate a Small Area of Your Home to Storing Extra Groceries.* The argument I often hear when I suggest people practice the Buy-Ahead Principle is "But I don't have any space to stock up." Well, in very rare cases (say, if your family of six is living in a one-bedroom apartment!), I'd agree. But in most cases, there are plenty of nooks and crannies in your home you could use creatively to store extra nonperishable food and household supplies. Maybe you need to clear out some items you're not using to make room. Or maybe you could install some extra shelving in a closet. Perhaps you could store things under the bed or in a few boxes in the garage. Get creative, think outside the box, and I'm guessing you'll find someplace you can use!

- *Determine When Enough Is Enough.* It's extremely cost effective to Buy Ahead, but it's just as important to know when enough is enough. If you have mountains of unopened tubes of toothpaste falling down on top of you when you open up the bathroom cupboard, you probably don't need to go out and buy fifty-five more! Twice a year, I go through our stockpile of groceries and household items and pare down to the basics that will last us for four to eight weeks. This way, we never have an overabundance.

- *Don't Buy Thirty-five Bottles of Something If You've Never Tried the Brand Before.* If you've never tried Cheeseburgers and Cream shampoo before (I made that up; please tell me there truly isn't a shampoo like that!) and it's on a great sale and there's a good coupon out for it, I'd suggest you buy a bottle or two and determine whether you like it or not before you stock up for the rest of the year. It's not saving money if you get a sweet deal on 30 bottles of shampoo that sit under your bathroom sink for five years because no one will use them!

HOW DO I KNOW IF IT'S A GOOD DEAL?

When you first begin attempting to cut your grocery bill, it can be daunting. It's all new and you have no idea if a "Sale" sign is truly a sale or just a gimmick. If you're overwhelmed and unsure about what constitutes a good deal, stick with the 40 percent to 75 percent off rule of thumb. If an item you typically buy is 40 percent to 75 percent off its retail price, go ahead and consider it a good deal for you and stock up—if you have the money in your budget. After all, if you're used to paying full price for most things you buy, then you're definitely going to save money if you focus on planning your menu around things that are 40 percent to 75 percent off.

"STACK" MANUFACTURER'S COUPONS AND STORE COUPONS

At the top of most coupons, there is a box with the date and a spot that says "Store Coupon" or "Manufacturer's Coupon." If it says "Store Coupon," it is a coupon produced by the store (depending upon the store, these are available on a store's website or in their store fliers) and it is viewed in the same way a sale at the store would be viewed, meaning you can use a manufacturer's coupon in addition to the store coupon on one item.

In other words, if you buy a box of crackers at Target for $2.50 and there is both a store coupon on the Target website for 50¢ off and a manufacturer's coupon from the newspaper for $1 off, you'll be able to use both coupons on one box of crackers and get $1.50 off the $2.50 price, making it only $1 after coupons for the box of crackers. When you use both a store coupon and a manufacturer's coupon on one item like this, it is called coupon "stacking." This is a perfectly legal and ethical way to get exceptional deals with coupons.

The only time you can use two coupons on one item is when you stack a manufacturer's coupon with a store coupon. You cannot use two store coupons or two manufacturer's coupons on the same item.

USE OVERAGE TO YOUR ADVANTAGE

When you become adept at using coupons, there are occa-sionally opportunities to purchase items that actually will be more than free. We call this "overage" in the coupon world. It typically happens when you have a coupon that exceeds the value of the item or when you purchase an item that trig-gers a coupon that is good on your next order.

Let's say you have a coupon for $3 off a box of dryer sheets and the dryer sheets are on sale for $2.33. Some stores will just "adjust down" the coupon value to take off $2.33 instead of $3 when they scan your coupon. Other stores will apply the "overage"—the negative 67¢ that is left after taking off the $2.33 for the box of dryer sheets—toward the rest of your groceries. Sixty-seven cents might not seem like much, but if you were to collect five $3-off coupons and buy five boxes of dryer sheets, you could get over $3 in overage to apply to your other groceries. Even if your family doesn't use dryer sheets, if you're going to be at the store anyway and you have five coupons, you might as well buy five boxes, donate or give away the dryer sheets, and use the overage toward some of your other groceries—like a gallon of milk or some fresh produce!

There are also ways to get items for "free-plus-overage," as we call it in the couponing world. That is when you com-bine a coupon with a sale that then also produces a catalina. What's that, you say? Well, it's just a fancy name for the cou-pons that are "$XX off your next order." The little machines that print these coupons are manufactured by the Catalina

Marketing company, which is the reason we couponers have dubbed them "catalinas."

Different manufacturers run specials throughout the year on certain products where you'll earn $XX amount off your next purchase when you buy two or more of an item. For instance, there was a deal recently where if you purchased four packages of Duracell batteries at $1.89 per package, you'd get a $3 catalina back. There were also $1.50-off coupons available at the time, so you could do the following:

1. Buy four packages of Duracell batteries at $1.98 each.

2. Use four $1.50-off coupons.

3. Spend $1.92 plus tax out of pocket and get back a $3 catalina good on your next order.

   In essence, you're getting the batteries free plus making around $1 extra in overage.

   You can also usually roll these deals, meaning, you can use the $3 catalina you earned to purchase four more packages of batteries plus $1 worth of other items, use the $3 catalinas to pay, spend basically nothing out of pocket, and get back another $3 catalina. If you have enough coupons and your store has plenty of stock, you could buy batteries to last you for the next six months or a year and pay literally nothing out of pocket, plus have extra money to put toward other groceries!

PUTTING IT ALTOGETHER: HOW TO USE YOUR GREAT DEALS TO FEED YOUR FAMILY

Learning to save money by using coupons is wonderful, but you'll truly save money only if you can practically apply this knowledge. Meaning, it's great to get twenty-five cans of tomato sauce for free, but if you don't do anything with that tomato sauce, you've wasted your time and effort. If your cupboards and refrigerator are stuffed to overflowing with great deals, but you're ordering pizza for dinner because you don't know how to prepare dishes based upon the items you purchased at rock-bottom prices, you've got a problem.

YOU NEED A PLAN

It's vitally important that you learn how to plan a menu based upon what's on sale at the store and what you have on hand. Menu planning ensures that you actually use the stuff you buy—and it also guarantees you have items on hand to make complete meals. This saves extra trips to the store and helps you avoid unplanned trips to the drive-through lane.

Menu planning doesn't just save you money; it also saves you time, effort, and stress. Planning a menu eradicates the dreaded "What's for dinner?" It allows you to kiss good-bye those last-minute frazzled dashes to the store throwing random items into your cart hoping it will magically turn into a five-course dinner.

GET THE BEST BANG FOR YOUR BUCK: PLAN A MENU BASED ON WHAT'S ON SALE AND WHAT YOU HAVE ON HAND

1. *"Shop" Your Cupboards.* Look in your freezer, refrigerator, and cupboards. This simple exercise often yields a great deal of inspiration. If you open up your freezer and find a bag of chicken and a bag of frozen broccoli and you open up your cupboard and see a bag of rice, that could be the beginnings of a Chicken Broccoli Rice Casserole. Just add cheese and cream of chicken soup to your grocery list and one dinner is taken care of.

2. *Consult the Sales Fliers.* When you're in the middle of planning your menu and grocery list, quickly browse through your weekly grocery store sale fliers (most grocery stores have their weekly sale fliers available online) and see if there are any exceptional deals on things you need or things you will use in the next few months. Most of the time, the hottest deals of the week are listed prominently on the front page of the flier. The more you can plan your menu based upon what is on a great sale rather than going by whatever sounds good, the more you will save. Once you decide which ingredients are on a great sale, incorporate these into your menu as much as you can. For instance, if chuck roasts are 50 percent off, then put roast on the menu. Or, if you see that apples are on sale for 99¢ a pound, it's the week for making apple pie.

3. **Survey Your Coupons.** After you have a good idea of what's on hand and what's on sale, pull out your coupons and look for any that match up with items you were planning to buy or that would make a great sale even sweeter. In many cases, a sale might not be that great, but when you can match a coupon with the sale, it becomes a fabulous deal. For example, this past week our Kroger affiliate store had Ronzoni pasta on sale for 89¢ per box when you bought 10 boxes. That's an okay deal, as far as pasta goes, but nothing spectacular. However, I had six coupons for $1 off two boxes of Ronzoni pasta (some from the newspaper and some I'd printed out online), so I was able to get 12 boxes of Ronzoni pasta for just 39¢ per box after the sale and the coupons.

4. **Make Your Final Menu Plan and Grocery List.** Using your list of recipe ideas and what's on sale at the store, create your final menu plan and grocery list for the week.

STRUGGLING TO COME UP WITH MEAL IDEAS?

- Create a list of thirty meals your family loves. When you're lacking inspiration, you can just whip out the list and have some instant ideas of family favorites.

- Have a recipe idea folder. Make a file in your filing cabinet to stick recipe ideas you come across in magazines, newspapers, and on food packages, and keep a running list on your computer of recipes you find online.

- Find inspiration online. Use AllRecipes.com, SuperCook
  .com, or RecipeMatcher.com to find recipes based on ingredients you already have on hand.

HAVE I MENTIONED HOW IMPORTANT IT IS TO TAKE IT SLOWLY?

One of the biggest mistakes new couponers make when they discover paying pennies on the dollar is they get so excited about all the money they are saving that they go a little overboard. Pretty soon, they burn out completely and go back to spending large amounts at the grocery store each week.

The better approach is to take it slowly. Pick and choose the best deals to work and don't worry about hitting the others. There will always be another sale on milk and cereal or whatever else seems like such a great deal at the time. Pace yourself and you'll find that you enjoy it a lot more. Don't try to cut your grocery bill by 50 percent right off the bat. Slowly reducing it bit by bit will set you up for long-term success.

And make sure that you focus on how much you are spending, not how much you are saving. It's fun to track your savings on your receipts, but don't get sucked into thinking you're saving money when you are really just "spaving" (i.e., spending money to save money). Seventy-five percent savings on your grocery bill may sound impressive, but the 25 percent spent is what matters most.

Stick to your grocery budget—even when it means passing up good deals—and you'll see much greater savings in the long run. In addition, realize that it's okay to step back and take a break every now and then. Sometimes, I'll shelve my Coupon Box for a week—or even a month!—and just do my shopping at Aldi (a discount grocery chain). It's better to pace yourself and stick with saving 40 percent on your grocery bill on a regular basis than to try to save 75 percent for two weeks and then get so burnt out that you go and blow your grocery budget for the next four weeks.

CHAPTER SEVEN

TWENTY-FIVE WAYS TO LOWER YOUR GROCERY BILL WITHOUT CLIPPING COUPONS

You'll save a lot of money using coupons, but that's not the only way to save on your grocery bill. You can save even more by implementing some or all of these 25 additional ways to keep your grocery budget under control.

1. Frequent the Dollar Store

Dollar stores can offer a treasure trove of bargains. They usually have great prices on spices as well as plastic bags. I also buy Nature's Own sandwich bread and hamburger buns for just $1 each at the Dollar Store—which is more than 50 percent off what I'd pay at the grocery store. Do note that not all stores with "dollar" in their name sell everything for $1 each. Also, some dollar store prices are actually more than what you'd pay at the grocery store. Consult the phone book and visit local dollar stores to check the prices against your price book (see page 202) and see if you'd save by making a stop at the dollar store on occasion.

2. Don't Be Brand Dependent

I'm not saying you need to give up all your favorite brands and go generic for everything. In fact, if you learn how to use coupons effectively, you can buy your favorite name-brand items often for pennies on the dollar by combining coupons with sales. However, if you are willing to base most of your purchases on the price rather than the brand, your pocketbook will thank you.

For example, let's say you are running low on shampoo. If you're stuck on buying only name-brand shampoo, the cheapest you may be able to buy it for (without using coupons) is $3 per bottle when it's on sale. If, however, you're willing to look for the lowest price on any brand of shampoo, you probably will be able to find shampoo priced at $1 per bottle on sale (without coupons). While the savings of $2 per bottle of shampoo might not seem too significant, think about how the savings could add up if you saved $2 on 15 different items each week at the grocery store because you chose price over brand. That would be a savings of $120 per month—or $1,440 per year!

3. Buy in Bulk

Buying grains, dried beans, as well as many other basic ingredients with long storage lives in large quantities will usually save you at least 20 percent, if not more. You can go in with a few friends and split the costs if you don't have enough storage space or money in the budget. It is also normally much more cost effective to purchase meat and staple ingredients in bulk. Call around to local farmers and see what they would charge you for purchasing a quarter or half of a cow. In many cases, it's at least $1 cheaper per pound to purchase in bulk. Search online or look in the phone book for nearby bulk food stores or co-ops that allow you to buy items in quantity. Remember always to check the price per ounce at your local grocery store, though, as just because it's a bulk quantity does not mean it's necessarily less expensive.

4. Use a Crock Pot

A crock pot can be one of the greatest tools in your money-saving, timesaving arsenal. You can pop ingredients for dinner in it in the morning and have a hot meal all ready by 5:00 p.m. Many of the newer crock pots even have time-delay features on them so that you can set them to turn on later in the day.

Fix It and Forget It *is a cookbook filled with crock pot recipe ideas—from soups to main dishes to sides to desserts. I also love the blog Crockpot365.blogspot .com, which chronicles Stephanie O'Dea's goal of using her crock pot every day for a year. There are over 365 crock pot recipes, complete with pictures and detailed instructions.*

5. Have a Meatless Night Once a Week

"Meatless" doesn't have to mean calorie-free or tasteless! When my husband and I were living on a beans-and-rice budget while he was in law school, we couldn't afford to buy a lot of meat. We often served breakfast foods for dinner. Or we'd have vegetable soup and bread. I also learned some recipes that I could eliminate the meat from and they'd still be flavorful—like lasagna, baked ziti, and bean burritos. It may take some creativity and a few flops to find out what meatless meals work for your family, but it might be worth the effort.

"A few years ago, I was looking at our grocery expenses for the previous year wondering how I could save money. I realized I was buying two packages of Hormel Black Label Bacon at $4.99 a package and using both each weekend. That's $10 a week or $520 a year we were spending on bacon. We really like bacon but not at that price. I started only buying it on sale, and we only ate it once a week on Sundays. I also cut each package in half and froze the other half. That made the price about $1.25 for each meal when I got it on sale for $2.50 per package. By doing this, we've saved $450.00 each year."

—Naomi, MoneySavingMom.com reader

---

6. Bake Your Own Bread (with a Bread Machine!)

I rarely buy bread other than sandwich bread and buns these days. Why would I when I can dump the ingredients in the bread machine, choose the dough setting, and push the button? Within an hour and a half, a beautifully raised lump of dough is ready to be formed into rolls, cinnamon rolls, a loaf of bread, French bread, or cinnamon raisin bread!

Instead of spending $2 to $4 on a loaf of store-bought bread or a pan of cinnamon rolls, I can whip up fresh bread for around 50¢ in just minutes using fresh, wholesome ingredients. In about five minutes, I'm saving $1 or $2 and making something really yummy and healthful for my family. That's the equivalent of saving $12 to $24 dollars per hour. And it's something I enjoy doing. If I were making bread by hand, I'd rarely make it because the mixing and kneading takes work and time. But the bread machine makes it super simple. Of course, the initial investment of a bread machine can be pricey. However, you can check local thrift stores, garage sales, or Craigslist to find one that is very inexpensive.

You can also let the bread machine do all the work of baking the loaf for you, but I've found that the loaf and crust tend to be harder when baked in the bread machine instead of baked in the oven. And it only takes a minute or two to transfer the dough from the bread machine to the loaf pan, so I prefer to bake the bread in the oven.

Tip: I have delicious recipes for Bread Machine Bread, Buttery Rolls, Cinnamon Swirl Bread, and Cinnamon Rolls in the recipe section on my blog, MoneySaving Mom.com.

If you've never used a bread machine before, I'd suggest borrowing one to make sure it is something that will work for you before you go out and invest in one. Consider asking for one for your birthday or Christmas, if you have a generous relative who likes buying kitchen gadgets for you! Or you can start by investing in an inexpensive one (Walmart carries some models for under $100). If you make two loaves of bread each week, the machine will pay for itself in around a year. And if you use it to make other types of breads—like cinnamon rolls and cinnamon swirl bread—the machine will pay for itself much faster!

Tip: If you end up making a lot of bread, you'll want to find a source for bulk yeast as it's outrageously expensive at the grocery store. Costco and Sam's Club both have the best prices I've found. If you don't have a membership, you can usually go with someone who does. Sam's Club also offers one day per year where non-members can get in free. If stored in the freezer, yeast will keep for at least a year.

7. Shop at the Bread Outlet

If you don't have a bread machine or you prefer store-bought bread for sandwiches, bread outlet stores are a way to get bread for at least 50 percent off the retail price. These stores usually sell discounted bread, hamburger and hot dog buns, English muffins, bagels, and other packaged bakery goods that will expire in a few days. You can stop by the bread store once a month and buy enough bread to last for the next four weeks. Put the bread in the freezer as soon as you arrive home and it should be good for up to six weeks after purchasing it.

8. Look for Marked-Down Groceries

I save a great deal of money every month by buying marked-down groceries. These are typically soon-to-be-expiring items (dairy products, meat, and produce). Not all stores offer markdowns, and store policies can vary widely. The best way to find out is to ask the produce manager what they do with produce, dairy, or meat products that are nearing their expiration dates.

I've scoped out all our nearby stores and know the best times to find markdowns, so I try to plan my shopping trips accordingly. The very first thing I do when I walk into a grocery store is to go around the perimeter of the store and look for the orange markdown stickers on items. I hit the produce section first. Then the meat, dairy, and bread items. By starting my shopping trip with looking for markdowns, I then can rework my grocery list if I hit on a great deal.

For example, let's say I was planning to buy carrots and cucumbers for sides for lunches on our menu that week. However, when I walked around looking for markdowns first thing after I got into the store, I found a big bag of marked-down colored peppers and cauliflower that were $2 less than the carrots and cucumbers I was planning to buy. By swapping raw peppers and cauliflower for the cucumbers and carrots on our menu, we'd save $2.

My favorite thing about buying markdowns is that they add some variety to our menu. You never know what you might find marked down that week and it's always fun to see if there's a way I can work it into the menu and substitute it for something I was planning to buy. Over the years, I've stumbled upon all sorts of interesting finds that have added extra pizzazz to our menus—and saved us money at the same time!

By the way, just because an item isn't marked down doesn't mean you can't get it discounted. Unless your store has a strict policy against marking down items, don't hesitate to ask if the store will reduce that past-its-prime bag of apples or that expiring-in-three-days jug of milk. I've rarely been turned down when asking if a store will mark down an obviously-close-to-expiring item. And on a few occasions, they've even just given it to me free!

"I buy the majority of my all-natural, additive- and preservative-free groceries from salvage grocery stores in my area. Salvage grocery stores buy damaged items or items that are close to expiring (even if they're expired, most of them are still good) at a discount from other stores. They then resell them at very low prices. I leave these stores with grocery carts full of frozen organic meats, organic cheese and eggs, and more. Typically, I spend four times less than I would've spent had I paid full retail for my organic/natural products."

—Catherine, MoneySavingMom.com reader

9. Use Half the Recommended Amount

You don't need to use the recommended amount of laundry detergent,[9] dish soap, or even shampoo! In most cases, much less will do. Train yourself to use two-thirds of the amount you usually do and you'll save 33 percent. Use half the amount you usually do, and you instantly start saving 50 percent!

Tip: Maybe this is going to sound over-the-top frugal, but it was a trick my mom taught me: when the bottle has almost been used up, add some water, put the lid back on, and shake it up to get the last remains of laundry detergent, salad dressing, dish soap, or whatever the bottle contains cleaned out of the bottle.

10. Serve Meat as a Condiment

I shamelessly stole this idea from Mary Ostyn's cookbook *Family Feasts for $75 a Week* because it's so brilliant. Serving meat in soup or on pizza is going to be a lot less expensive than serving roast and sirloin, especially if you're buying high-quality meat. If you don't want to try a meatless meal each week, at least try one or two meat-as-a-condiment meals. You can often cut the meat by 30 percent to 50 percent in most soups, casseroles, pizza, and so many other things without anyone really noticing.

---

[9] http://www.nytimes.com/2010/03/13/your-money/13shortcuts.html?pagewanted=1&_r=1&ref=general&src=me.

"With two teenagers who can eat seven to eight tacos each, this relatively inexpensive food was becoming out of reach when fixed with ground beef or even chicken! I started using 3/4 part lentils mixed with 1/4 part ground beef for the taco meat mixture. The spices and bit of ground beef cover any 'beany' lentil flavor. My family loves it and now I can afford for them to eat seven tacos each!"

—Susan, MoneySavingMom.com reader

11. Stick with Simple Meals That Use Inexpensive Ingredients

When you're planning your menu, think about how much your recipes will cost you to make. It doesn't have to be a scientific to-the-penny figure, but just having a good idea that there is a $10 difference between the price of making one meal as opposed to another meal can help you decide whether you can afford to make certain meals regularly or whether you should save them for special occasions only.

12. Eat from the Pantry

On occasion, challenge yourself to see how long you can go without going to the grocery store. When we do this, I often find we have a lot more food on hand than I realized. And I get creative and start pulling things out of the back of the cupboard or freezer and concocting new recipes and meals.

Tip: MyFridgeFood.com will help you make meals out of items you already have on hand.

13. Use Bone-In Chicken Breasts

If you prefer white meat, you can save quite a bit by buying bone-in chicken breasts versus boneless, skinless chicken breasts. You just cut a simple bone off and you have a boneless chicken breast—for 30 percent off what you'd pay for boneless, skinless chicken breasts.

14. Price-Match at Walmart and Target

Do you like the idea of shopping at multiple stores I shared in chapter 6 but you don't want to hassle with actually *going* to multiple stores? Walmart and Target both match competitors' prices. Just bring the competitor's ad in to verify the price. So if you see a great deal on grapes and bread at the grocery store ten miles away and Walmart is just two blocks away, bring the grocery store's ad to Walmart and get the same deals. Of course, if you load up your cart with other impulse purchases while you're at Walmart, it's not saving you any money!

15. Order Groceries Online

Most people are skeptical that you can truly save money by buying groceries online, but it's true. Since you should have already set up a price book (see chapter 6) and know the lowest prices you routinely pay at your local stores, it's easy to determine whether you'll save by ordering online. In fact, you can even put in the prices you routinely pay to Camel CamelCamel.com and they will track when the price goes below your desired price and send you an email. I've found Amazon.com, Soap.com, Diapers.com, and Alice.com sales to all be fairly competitive with local grocery store prices. As I come across these, I post them on my blog, MoneySaving Mom.com.

16. Use Your Freezer

I save so much money by using my freezer! I buy soon-to-be-expiring milk, cream cheese, meat, bread, fruit, shredded cheese, and more and freeze it for later use. If I find a great deal on fruit, I buy as much as I can afford in our grocery budget and then I freeze what we don't consume within a few days to use in smoothies. When I buy almost-expired milk, I freeze it to use in pancake and waffle batter. By stocking up on items when they are at great prices and then freezing them, it gives me more variety to work with when planning our menus and saves us money, too.

Batch cooking is another way I save a lot of money with our freezer. I often cook up a big batch of chicken breasts and chop and freeze them to use in soup, casseroles, on pizza, or in stir-fry. Or I'll make up taco meat, meatballs, or burrito filling for quick and easy dinners. Just cool and put these in zip-top freezer bags, make sure all the air is out, label, and freeze flat. When you're ready to use, just thaw it overnight in the refrigerator.

Put forth a little effort on a regular basis to make food in bulk and then freeze it. You'll find it's a huge relief and help to be able to whip up a meal in minutes using food you've pre-prepared and frozen. Plus, having food at-the-ready in the freezer also cuts down on the urge to grab something at a fast-food restaurant or order pizza on those days when you don't have time to cook dinner.

Tip: If you can devote an hour or two to prepping things for the freezer on the weekends, it will save you lots of time and work during the week. Or, if your week-ends are packed, consider making multiples of a meal at least one or two nights each week. It doesn't take much more effort to make a triple batch of meatballs, and then you have dinner covered plus two extra meals in the freezer! If you're new to freezer cooking and won-dering how to do it, you can find lots of freezer-cooking recipes and tips on LifeAsMom.com.

17. Don't Throw Out Your Leftovers

Creatively remaking your leftovers into tomorrow's lunch or dinner is a great way to stretch your budget and not waste food. Eating leftovers for lunch, instead of sandwiches, or serving a once-a-week Leftover Buffet (just set out all the leftovers from the fridge and let everyone dish up their own plates and heat them up in the microwave) are other options. LeftoverChef.com is a wonderful resource if you need ideas for recipes to make with your leftovers. You can choose what items you have and it will pull up recipes you can make.

> "Our leftovers were getting lost in the fridge, so we devised two new practices. First, we now have a dedicated shelf for leftovers. Secondly, we use a dry-erase marker to label the contents of the containers. No more finding last month's lasagna in the back corner of the bottom shelf or wondering what's in that blue container."
>
> —Cyndi, MoneySavingMom.com reader

18. Make Your Own Homemade Cleaners

You can save a lot of money by making your own cleaners and laundry soap. While we don't make all our cleaners, I have used baking soda for many a stubborn job. In addition, we've recently been experimenting with homemade dish-washing detergent and homemade laundry soap. MomsBudget.com has an extensive list of homemade cleaner recipes if you'd like to try making them yourself.

Tip: If you don't want to give up dryer sheets but you want to make them last longer, you can cut them in half or fourths and just use one strip per load. It's still as effective!

19. Eliminate Paper Products

Disposable products are very handy, and they make life easier, but they certainly aren't inexpensive. We've not completely eliminated all disposable products from our home; we still occasionally use paper plates and napkins and, of course, we use toilet paper. We have learned, however, that you can live just fine without pretty much all paper products but toilet paper (we're not planning on giving that up any time soon!). We exclusively cloth-diapered for two and a half years, we've used rags instead of paper towels for many years, and we've gone for long stretches of time without buying any paper plates, napkins, or cups.

Tip: If you're not ready to give up paper towels completely, try cutting the roll in half down to the tube. Then, instead of using a full paper towel, you'll find most jobs only require half a sheet.

"I cut up my husband's old tee-shirts and use them in place of paper towels. They work better than paper towels at cleaning up messes, and they are easy to wash. If a mess is particularly icky, I simply throw away the rag. I have no problem doing so since the tee-shirt was destined for the trash anyway."

—Becky, MoneySavingMom.com reader

20. Ditch Cereal for Breakfast

Cereal can be a budget buster. Most boxes of cereal are at least $3 each and when you add in milk to pour over the cereal, breakfast of cereal for a family of five can easily cost close to $5. Multiply that by 7, and you're looking at $35 per week spent on breakfast! If you're shopping with coupons, you can often get cereal for as low as $1 per box—or even less—but if you don't want to mess with coupons or you like the idea of feeding your family a wholesome and nutritious homemade breakfast very inexpensively, here are some ideas:

- *Pancakes, Waffles or French Toast.* As mentioned above, I'm often able to get milk marked down half price when it's nearing its expiration date. I buy it and we use what we can before the expiration date, and then I stick it in the freezer. When I have an extra hour or two and the motivation, I pull out the frozen milk, thaw it, and use it to make a quadruple batch of homemade pancakes or waffles to stick in the freezer. These are so handy to have on hand and make for quick and easy breakfasts: just pull the waffles or pancakes you need out of the freezer, pop them in the microwave or toaster oven, and you have a delicious and very inexpensive hot breakfast to serve. We like to add in some chocolate chips to the pancake batter and then skip the syrup.
- *Instant Oatmeal Packets.* Instead of buying expensive individual instant oatmeal packets, make your own! A quick Google search will bring up a plethora of recipes and add-in ideas.
- *Smoothies.* Smoothies are delicious and nutritious. Plus, if you buy fruit when it's marked down or on a great sale

and then freeze it, smoothies are rather inexpensive—
especially when compared to the prices you'd pay at
Smoothie King or Jamba Juice!

- *Homemade Granola.* We like to serve homemade granola over yogurt with some fresh fruit. If yogurt is on
  sale and you buy fruit in season, this can be a very eco-
  nomical breakfast!

21. Invest in Reusable Water Bottles

If you occasionally buy disposable water bottles, you can save
a lot of money by investing in reusable water bottles for each
family member. You can find them for a dollar at the dollar
store. Just wash, fill, and refrigerate and you'll save at least
10¢ to 50¢ (or more!) each time you use them instead of a
disposable water bottle.

22. Shop Every Other Week

I've found that the less I shop, the less I spend. Challenge
yourself to shop every other week or every ten days for a
two-month period and see if it affects your grocery bill, too!

23. Buy Roast on Sale and Have It Ground

Buy lean cut bottom round roast on sale and have it ground
at the meat counter. This makes excellent 90 percent to 95
percent lean ground beef and it's usually quite a bit less than
you'd pay for high-quality ground beef.

Our store sells turkeys for around 19¢ a pound in November. I stock up on twelve of the largest turkeys I can find! I pull one out of the freezer each month, and cook it. I can get six to eight meals from one $3 turkey!"

—Jennifer, MoneySavingMom.com reader

24. Buy Produce in Season and on Sale

We plan our menu based upon what's in season and on sale. While this means we don't always have twenty-three different kinds of fruits and vegetables on hand, it saves money and allows us to enjoy what's fresh and seasonal during each particular month and season. If a fruit or vegetable is on sale that can be frozen or will stay fresh for longer than a week, I try to buy extra to freeze or to enjoy the following week.

25. Plant a Garden

Produce is typically only pennies per item from your own backyard, it's tremendously fresh, and you know exactly what you did or didn't spray on it. Plus, you can freeze or can your extras—or bless your friends and neighbors with them! Have a brown thumb? Find a friend who loves gardening and trade services (babysitting, bread baking, car maintenance?) in exchange for their garden excess.

Tip: Check LocalHarvest.org to find local farms that sell produce to the general public.

HOW MUCH ARE YOU SAVING PER HOUR?

If you're just learning how to reduce your grocery budget, don't try to do all these suggestions at once. Pick one or two to try implementing and experiment with each month. And remember to factor in the time spent versus the money saved. It is easy to get so caught up in trying to pinch every penny that we lose sight of the big picture. We can become so focused on trying to save money that we end up spending hours and hours and *hours* of time to save a mere few dollars.

Personally, if I'm not saving at *least* $20 per hour by implementing a particular frugal practice, then I'd rather invest my time elsewhere. Of course, this rule doesn't apply if it's something I really enjoy doing. However, if I'm doing something primarily for the money saved, then it is important to me that I'm actually *saving money!*

For instance, I don't make my own homemade tortillas. This confession sometimes shocks people. But after making my own tortillas, I realized it wasn't worth my time for the small amount of money saved. You see, I can pick up a package of eight to ten tortillas at the store for around $1 whereas making them from scratch costs 30¢ to 40¢ per batch. Yes, homemade tortillas are slightly less expensive than store bought tortillas. However, to make eight to ten tortillas from start to finish takes me around thirty minutes. At that rate, I'd be spending thirty minutes of my time to save around 60¢ to 70¢ total. Even if I figured out a way to make them more efficiently and somehow could whip out seventy tortillas from start to finish in an hour, I'd still only be saving less than $5 for an hour's worth of work. At this season of life, my time is more valuable than saving less than minimum wage per hour.

CHAPTER EIGHT

GOING OUT ON THE TOWN WITHOUT GOING BROKE

Most people have this idea that living on a budget means you can never have fun. "Frugal living" is somehow equated with miserly living—people who dress in drab and dreary clothing, eat ninety-nine variations of beans and rice dishes, and whittle away their days counting the pennies they've saved through leading a dull and miserable existence.

This couldn't be further from the truth! Living on a budget allows you to plan for strategic splurging. If you're on a tight budget, a "splurge" might be dinner at a fast-food restaurant once every other month or picking up pizza and a movie. If you have more wiggle room, you might be able to do something on a larger scale occasionally.

When you follow the steps I outlined in the previous chapters and have a plan in place for your life and your money, you are in a position to dictate where your money goes instead of the money dictating where you go and what you do. You can carefully choose your priorities when it comes to money: you can choose to save in areas that don't matter to you so that you can spend in areas that do matter. You can choose to cut back in some areas, so you can spend in others. When you become the master of your minutes and your money, it frees you up to enjoy life like never before!

We eat out once a week, we enjoy family vacations, we enjoy fun family outings, and we strategically splurge on things that are important to us. That said, as much as is possible, we follow this rule:

RULE #6: NEVER PAY RETAIL

There are so many ways to enjoy life—at a discount! When you commit to never paying retail, it opens up a world of creative ideas and possibilities. Here are a few to get you started:

How to Eat Out on a Budget

- *Look at the Price First.* Instead of looking at the menu and deciding what you want to eat and then looking at the price and deciding whether or not you can afford it, start by deciding what your budget is for your restaurant dinner and then look at the prices to figure out which menu items are within your range.
- *Use Coupons.* A coupon for a free entree when you purchase another can definitely save you a nice chunk of money—especially if the restaurant has entrees priced at $10 or less. Also, look for coupons for 25 percent off your entire bill. CouponCravings.com has the latest printable coupons available for restaurants nationwide.

TWO WAYS TO GET GIFT CARDS FOR CHEAP—OR FREE!

1. **Buy Them at a Discount.** You can purchase discounted gift cards online from CityDeals.com, GiftCards.com, GiftCardRescue.com, or eBay. They are typically discounted by $5 to $10. It's not much, but it can stretch your dollar just a little further.

2. **Earn Them for Free.** You can earn free gift cards through Swagbucks.com and MyPoints.com. Swagbucks gives you the opportunity to earn points toward gift cards and other prizes by doing web searches, watching videos, filling out surveys, or taking polls. You can also earn points by referring others. You can earn points toward gift cards from MyPoints.com by reading emails, placing online orders through their website, printing coupons, and more.

- *Look for "Kids Eat Free" Deals.* If you have children, go to restaurants where children eat free with a paying adult. Some restaurants offer this all the time, others offer it on select evenings. KidsMealDeals.com allows you to search for Kids Eat Free deals in your local area. You can also Google your city name and "kids eat free" to see what it brings up. Call your store ahead of time to verify they are offering free kids' meals with an adult purchase as deals may change or vary from location to location.

- *Order Water.* Water might be boring, but choosing it over other drinks at a restaurant can save you a big chunk. MoneySavingMom.com reader, Lorie, says: "If your family of four orders water instead of $1.99 soft drinks and you go out to eat once a month, you will save around $96 per year. Add in the extra 15 percent tip you'd pay for the soft drinks and you're saving over $100 each year just by ordering water!"

- *Go Out for Dessert or Coffee.* When we were living on a really tight budget and eating out was a very rare occasion, we loved to have bookstore dates. I'd earn a $5 gift card to a local bookstore through MyPoints.com (usually from reading hundreds of their daily points-earning emails) and then we'd go out and browse books and split a fancy coffee. It felt so extravagant and yet it cost us nothing out of pocket! A few years later, when we weren't quite so poor, we started having weekly dessert dates. We found a sit-down restaurant that sold delicious and generously portioned desserts for just $5. We'd split one and could eat out for under $10, including the tip. We'd go the hour before closing so that we weren't holding up a table during the busy dinner hour rush. It was so leisurely and luxurious to have weekly family date nights at a sit-down restaurant, but we were able to do it quite economically.

SHORT ON CASH?
HAVE A LOOSE CHANGE DATE!

During our first few years of marriage—when money was extremely tight—we put any extra pennies, nickels, or dimes into a change cup that we kept in our kitchen cupboard. When we were feeling particularly burnt out and in dire need of a pick-me-up, we'd take the change cup to the bank and exchange it for dollar bills. You know that money was tight because usually after a year of putting in our extra pennies, nickels, and dimes, all we'd have would be around $7 to $8 collected! But that $7 to $8 could mean we could rent a movie at the dollar movie store and get dinner at a fast-food restaurant with coupons. And you know what? A little splurge like that often did the trick to reinvigorate us on our frugal journey.

- *Learn to Love the Dollar Menu.* The Dollar Menu is every frugal family's best friend! Should I admit that we know exactly what each fast-food restaurant in our city has on their Dollar Menu? And it's always a sad day if they decide to move something from their dollar menu and start charging more than a dollar for it! We love that we can go and get a treat for everyone (we usually tell the children that they can have any one item they'd like to choose off the dollar menu) without making much of a dent in our Eating Out cash envelope.

- *Sign Up for Birthday Freebies.* If you haven't taken advantage of all the wonderful freebies available on or around your birthday, you are completely missing out! You can get free ice cream from multiple places, free meals from a number of different restaurants, and more. Now, of course, these are only a good deal if you don't bring the whole family and blow the budget while you're getting your free birthday meal! My two favorite birthday freebies are the $5 gift card from Jason's Deli and the free drink of your choice from Starbucks. (You have to register a Starbucks card to get this, so be sure to do so if you earn one from Swagbucks.com or someone gives you one as a gift!) You can find an extensive and frequently updated list of birthday freebies to sign up for at http://MoneySavingMom.com/birthday-freebies.

Tip: Want to enjoy the restaurant experience without the expense? Try your hand at making restaurant food at home! RecipeZaar.com has a section with many different restaurant copycat recipes.

SKIP PIZZA DELIVERY AND
MAKE YOUR OWN!

One simple and extremely delicious way to save money is to skip ordering pizza for your family and make your own. If you're anything like us, you'll probably never go back to frozen or restaurant pizza again! Truth be told, we've ordered pizza only two times in all nine years of our marriage, and we both agree that homemade pizza is so much better! Here's my favorite pizza dough recipe:

Homemade Pizza
Pizza Crust
   1 Tbsp. active dry yeast
   1 cup warm water (105° to 115° F.)
   1 tsp. sugar
   1 tsp. salt
   2 Tbsp. vegetable oil
   2½ cups flour

Dissolve the yeast in the water. Add the rest of the ingredients in and mix. Dump onto a floured surface. Knead into a smooth dough (five minutes or so). Roll out and press down onto a greased pizza pan. Add toppings of your choice. Have fun and be creative with this. The possibilities are practically endless! Our favorite variety is salsa or barbecue sauce, diced cooked chicken, and cheese. Bake at 450° F. for around 12 to 15 minutes until the crust looks crispy and lightly browned.

How to Save Money on Family Fun and Entertainment

- *Use Your Local Library.* Most libraries offer much more than books: they have free classes, free internet, free movies, free CDs, free ebooks, free audiobooks, and more to check out. Some even have admission tickets to local attractions and museums that you can check out and use to get in for free. Plus, even if your local library doesn't have a huge selection of books, most can get almost any book if you request it through interlibrary loan. Libraries also have fun summer reading programs with prizes that children—and adults!—can participate in.

- *Purchase Memberships or Season Tickets.* If you are going to go to a museum, amusement park, or other venue at least three times in a year, it usually is a better deal to purchase a membership or season tickets. This is a bigger cost upfront, but it saves you quite a bit down the line. Plus, you can go as many times as you want without having to worry about the cost! This is also a great gift idea to request from grandparents for Christmas—or even to buy for your own family as a family Christmas gift.

- *Take Advantage of Free Events.* Almost all towns, cities, and counties have free events. Pick up a local parents' magazine and check the listings for area festivals, parades, classes, and other activities.
- *Watch Movies at Home.* Yes, I know, watching a movie at home just isn't as "exciting" as watching it on a big screen, but when you add up how much it costs to buy movie tickets these days, you'll quickly realize that you'll save a boatload of money by making going to the theater a rare treat rather than a regular occurrence. To save even more money, check out DVDs at the library or rent movies from Redbox or Blockbuster Express for $1 per night. You can find free Redbox rental codes at Inside Redbox.com.
- *Watch TV Online.* I'm constantly amazed when people tell me they don't have time to do a budget or clip coupons or start an online business and yet they somehow keep up with all the latest TV shows. I don't think everything on TV is pointless and purposeless. There are some good shows, and it's important to keep up with current events. But I don't think it's necessary—or even healthful!—to spend hours each week sitting in front of a black box watching mindless shows. Not only that, but a cable package is expensive! The good news? With Hulu .com, Amazon Instant Video, and many television shows offering their episodes online, you don't need to pay for a cable package and you can still enjoy a few shows each week—and save yourself a bundle of money!
- *Listen to Music Online.* Try Pandora, Rhapsody, Grooveshark, or other free streaming services. Instead

of downloading songs off of iTunes, you can listen to music online. Pandora is an online radio station with free live streaming. Just type in a style of music you enjoy, and it will program a station for you. You can even create your own station that mixes a variety of different styles. If you want to choose your specific songs, Grooveshark. com allows you to create your own free music stream with songs you've handpicked.

- *Swap Your Books.* If you love reading, PaperBackSwap (PBS) is a perfect way to add new books to your library on a dime. You just find books in your home that you no longer need, list them on PBS, and, when you ship one out to another PBS member, you receive a book credit that you can use toward any book on PaperBackSwap .com. To get you started, they give you two free book credits when you list your initial ten books. For best results, create a wish list of books you want to add to your home library on PBS. You'll be notified as soon as a book on your wish list is posted and you'll have forty-eight hours to request it before it goes into the general system. Shipping is under $3 for most books, so it can end up being much less expensive than paying for books you want to buy. PaperBackSwap also has two sister sites: Swap-A-DVD and Swap-A-CD, which work very much the same for DVDs and CDs.

VOLUNTEER AND GET IN FREE

"We are heading to the National Wildlife and Turkey Federation Convention soon. The tickets cost $20 each, but all four of us will get in free. No, we are not sneaking in; we will have nametags and be welcomed at the registration desk because we are volunteering! For the exchange of three hours' worth of work, we get admission to this large convention. This principle has worked for numerous other events that we have wanted to attend, but just could not come up with the money."

—Dee, MoneySavingMom.com reader

How to Save Money on Vacations

- *Go During the Off Season.* The difference in price between off-season rates and normal rates for hotels and attractions can be staggering. In addition to saving money, when you go during the off-season, you avoid the crowds and long lines.
- *Purchase Tickets Through a Travel Site.* When booking airfare, hotels, or rental cars, always check multiple sites online for the best deal. I recommend Orbitz.com, Travelocity.com, Expedia.com, and Hotwire.com. Also, if you have some flexibility in your travel plans, try variations when searching—like staying a day later or arriving a day earlier. Sometimes changing the dates a little can mean big savings. Also, you'll usually find the best deals online if you purchase your tickets in the middle of the week instead of on the weekends.

"We are a family of eight and my husband is the youth pastor at our church. Because of his busy and often hectic schedule, we have decided that a yearly family vacation is going to be top priority. We budget $1,000 every year out of our tax returns to pay for our trip, but with such a large family, it can be a challenge to stay within our budget. We save on vacations by using the site vrbo .com (Vacation Rentals by Owners). We find a cabin or vacation home that we are interested in, and then we negotiate with the owners over the phone for a top-rate deal. Although owners post their own rates on the website, you can also contact them and make them an offer. Sometimes it has taken dozens of phone calls, but we've always eventually been able to find a rental within our budget, saving us hundreds of dollars on our vacation. Plus, because we stay in a cabin or vacation home with a kitchen, we are able to make most all of our own meals, instead of paying to eat out."

—Angela, MoneySavingMom.com reader

- *Get a Package Deal.* If you are flying somewhere, you'll normally save at least a few hundred dollars by purchasing a flight, hotel, and/or rental car together as a package deal through a travel site. Again, if you can be flexible on airlines and hotels, you will save a lot more. When you are ready to order, make sure to go through Ebates.com so that you get cash back on your order, too.

"I use Priceline's 'Name Your Own Price' any time I book a hotel. This on its own saves money, but I go one step further and use BiddingForTravel.com's Priceline message boards to learn what the most recent winning bids and hotels have been on Priceline! The website also has great strategies to help you get the most out of Priceline bidding."

—Kristi, MoneySavingMom.com reader

- *Bring Your Own Food.* If you are driving, bring as much food as you can and plan your meals out ahead of time. In addition, if you are planning to go to attractions, check and see if you can bring in your own food instead of paying for overpriced venue food and drinks.

- *Buy Food at the Grocery Store.* This is one of our favorite tricks—especially if I wasn't organized enough for us to bring a lot of food ahead of time! Instead of going to restaurants, we'll stop by the grocery store and pick up a bag of baby carrots, some apples, bread, peanut butter, jelly, and a box of granola bars. It might not be as exciting as Happy Meals, but it sure is less expensive—and it will usually feed us for a few lunches and snacks.

- *Use Coupons and Groupons.* When you are planning your trip, look for coupons and Groupons you can use in areas and cities you'll be in. If you're planning to go out to dinner, you might as well get 50 percent off!

GROUPON.COM: FOOD, FAMILY FUN, AND MORE—ON A DIME

Groupon.com is all the rage and there's a reason: you can score some amazing deals through it! However, with all things like this, you have to be careful. Just because it's a great deal doesn't mean you are going to save money if you won't use the deal and can't afford it. Here's how it works: Groupon works with local businesses all across the country to procure rock-bottom deals—usually to the tune of 50 percent to 75 percent off. They then offer this deal as a one-day special on the Groupon section of the site for your area and send out an email to everyone signed up for the deals for that area. You usually have twenty-four hours to purchase the deal—unless there's a cap on it (i.e., some companies choose to limit their deals to the first three hundred people who purchase it). Once you've purchased the deal, your "Groupon" will show up in your account under "My Groupons." You can print this or show it on your phone just like a coupon to get the deal.

It's very common for Groupon to offer a $30 restaurant voucher for $15. If you like the restaurant or you're game to try it soon, purchasing a voucher for half price or lower can be a great deal. Do be careful, though! Before purchasing, make sure you read all of the fine print and check the restaurant prices if it's somewhere you've never been before. If you get $20 off, but the restaurant charges $40 per plate, it's probably not going to save you any money. It's also tempting to purchase Groupons for things you usually wouldn't buy or services you usually wouldn't pay for just because it's such a "good deal" (after all, it can be hard to pass up a voucher for a pedicure at 75 percent off!). This is when sticking with a cash budget can be so helpful. If you have extra money in your Eating Out cash envelope, can afford that heavily discounted restaurant, and it's something you're sure you'll use, then go for it guiltlessly. But don't buy Groupons on your credit card and then end up not having enough money to pay for groceries!

How to Save Money on Clothing

- *Shop Your Wardrobe Before Going to the Mall.* When you feel like you don't have anything to wear, go through your closet and dresser before heading to the mall. Pull everything out and see if there are items you are no longer wearing that you could get rid of. In the process, you'll probably find a few things you like that you forgot you even owned. Plus, you may come up with some new outfit combinations and save yourself a shopping trip.

ARE YOU WEARING WHAT YOU ALREADY OWN?

Sometimes we don't even realize how few items we use. For instance, do you know how many clothes in your closet you are actually wearing? Probably fewer than you think! J. D. Roth, from the widely read Get Rich Slowly blog, did an experiment in 2010 to help him purge his closet of excess clothes. He moved all of his sweaters and button-down shirts to an unused closet. Then, when he needed a shirt to wear, he'd pull what he wanted to wear from the extra closet and add it to his regular closet. After nine months of doing this experiment, he discovered that there were only seventeen button-down shirts and three sweaters that he wore on a regular basis. And—get this—there were thirty shirts in the extra closet that he hadn't worn at all—for nine whole months!

He wrote about this experiment: "Sometimes I think I'm the village idiot. I don't even wear two-thirds of my wardrobe? It's like I'm just throwing my money away. But rather than beat myself up over this, I can use the info going forward."

- *Frequent Garage Sales.* Garage sales are a bargain shopper's gold mine! Have a running list of items you are needing/wanting to purchase so you know what to look for when shopping and don't just pick up something because it's a screaming deal. Check Craigslist.org before going out and map your route based upon what sales are advertising items of interest to you. Be sure to get to the best sales early, before things are picked over, and don't hesitate to make an offer if an item you are interested in is priced higher than you want to pay. Since you can't try things on in a fitting room or take something back for a return, bring a tape measure with you and a list of your family's clothing measurements to make sure clothing items will fit.

- *Go to Consignment Sales.* Many communities have annual consignment sales put on by groups of individuals or organizations. It's basically like a huge, well-organized garage sale, usually featuring children's clothing and toys, and it's an excellent way to find deals on children's clothing. The prices are normally reasonable, and the selection is usually massive. Most sales offer everything at half price the last day. You can also participate in the sale and make money off clothing your children no longer need or wear. You normally are required to help organize and set up the sale, possibly work a few hours during the sale, and then you earn a percentage of your items that sell. One of the side perks of selling at a consignment sale is that you usually get to shop during sneak-preview hours, so you have first dibs on the best deals and clothes.

- *Shop at Consignment Stores and Thrift Stores.* I prefer consignment stores and thrift stores over garage sales. They have more of a selection, and I don't have to drive around to multiple locations. Ask to be put on their mailing lists so you can be notified of sales and specials.

- *Host a Swap Party.* Amber, a MoneySavingMom.com reader, emailed me and said, "I save well over a hundred dollars a year by hosting mommy swap parties. I invite all my friends who have kids to come over and bring all their kids' outgrown clothes and toys. We lay all the items on blankets in my backyard and then we go shopping for free. We all walk away with lots of 'new' great items for our children."

- *Check the Clearance Racks.* When you walk into a department store, head straight for the clearance racks. Much of the time, you can find items that will work there without even looking at the regularly priced clothing.

- *Look at the Price Tag First.* When shopping, train yourself always to look at the price tag first. That way, you can walk away from something that isn't in your budget before you fall in love with it.

- *Do You Really Love It?* Always try on items before you buy them. Look in the dressing room mirror and ask yourself: "Do I love this? Does it fit well? Can I afford it? Do I have shoes to match?" I've put many, many items back on the rack over the years because I've not been able to answer "yes" to all these questions.

DRESS YOUR CHILDREN FOR FREE?

If you have children, consigning their clothes can be a great way to upgrade their wardrobe to a new size or season very inexpensively, especially if you aren't the recipient of a lot of hand-me-downs. Jessica, one of my blog readers, is a manager of a consignment store. She says, "Most shops offer at least 50 percent of the selling price, which is a really good deal. Sometimes they offer you a higher percentage if you use your income as store credit. Let's say you sell ten items and your total profit is $20 at 50 percent. If the store has a 75 percent store credit policy, this means if you spend your income in their store, they're actually giving you $30 instead of just $20!"

If you become proficient in consignment store shopping and like to shop at garage sales, you can maximize on the store credit bonus by purchasing items inexpensively at garage sales, having your children wear them for a season, and then trading them in at a consignment store for store credit. You may even be able to almost clothe your children for free or almost free some seasons by doing this!

However, be aware that many consignment stores have very strict rules on what they will accept. My friend, Jen, is a used–clothing store frequenter who blogs at BeautyandBedlam .com. She says, "Do not take it personally if the majority of your clothes are rejected at the consignment stores. With thrift shopping and 'frugal fashionistas' being on the rise, store owners have gotten increasingly picky to the point that many are only taking clothes that are less than two years old. But you can get some great prices for what they do take, so it's definitely worth a shot."

"I save more than $100 per year by buying my child's clothing at garage sales and consignment sales. I look for name-brand, high-quality clothing up to five sizes in advance, usually paying between 25¢ and $1 per item. After getting good use out of the clothing, I resell them at the twice-yearly consignment sales in my city. Often times, I make more than I originally paid for the clothes."

—Shannon, MoneySavingMom.com reader

How to Save Money on Glasses, Contacts, and Dental Work

- *Get Free or Low-Cost Exams at an Optometry or Dental School.* If there's an optometry or dental school in your area, find out if they offer services to the general public. MoneySavingMom.com reader Daisy says, "We get our annual eye examinations for free by having them done at our local optometry school. A student conducts the exam under close professional supervision, and the exam is extremely thorough." And reader Heidi says, "There is a community college near our home that has a dental hygiene program. By going there and having my teeth cleaned, checked, and any X-rays, I pay anywhere from $25 to $40 per visit (cleanings/check-ups are $25, X-rays are $10 to $20 more). This easily saves me $50 to $80 every six months over going to my own dentist. Plus the service at the clinic is very thorough and includes dental care teaching."

- *Order Glasses Through ZenniOptical*.com. Need a new pair of glasses? ZenniOptical.com offers prescription glasses for less than $20 shipped. We've ordered glasses from them multiple times and been more than pleased. It is a little difficult to know exactly what they'll look like on you from just a picture online, but if you're using them for reading glasses, or you're not extremely particular, I promise they'll work. Zenni Optical walks you through how to purchase the glasses and take the fitting and eye measurements. It's a simple process and so much less expensive than ordering from your local optometrist! In fact, while you'll usually spend at least $200 at the optometrist, you'll rarely spend more than $30 from Zenni Optical.

- *Buy from a Store That Specializes in Glasses.* If the thought of ordering glasses online is too far out of your comfort zone, you can still save quite a bit by buying them from a store like LensCrafters rather than from your local optometrist. Often, LensCrafters or similar stores will offer coupons in the Sunday paper. Before we discovered Zenni Optical, we bought our glasses this way—paying around $50 per pair after a coupon.

- *Order Contacts Online.* It's much less expensive to order contacts online through VisionDirect.com or 1800Contacts.com than it is to purchase them from your optometrist. Compare prices at both sites and look for a coupon code on RetailMeNot.com. Order through Ebates.com to get cash back as well.

- *Purchase at Sam's Club, BJ's, or Costco.* MoneySaving Mom.com reader Lindsey says, "I buy my prescription contacts at Sam's Club optical instead of from the eye doctor. It would cost me $37.50 per box to get my contacts from the eye doctor, and it's only $14 per box at Sam's Club. The savings really add up!"

How to Save Money on Utilities

- *Install a Programmable Thermostat.* Purchase an inexpensive programmable thermostat and set it a few degrees cooler for eight hours at night in the winter and a few degrees warmer at night in the summer. This can save you at least $15 to $25 per month on your utility bill, without any extra work or effort on your part.

- *Cancel All Unnecessary Services on Your Phone.* Do you need caller ID or call waiting or a long-distance plan? If not, don't pay for them. Want to get a little more radical? Consider ditching your landline altogether and switching to MagicJack or Skype. MoneySavingMom.com reader Tiffani says, "About a year ago we canceled our landline and bought a Skype phone from Amazon. We pay $5 per month for unlimited local and long distance calls. We were paying $30/month just for basic phone, so this is a savings of $25 per month or $300 a year."

"I recently switched my Verizon cell phone to Straight Talk, a no-contract cell phone company. For $30 a month, I get 1,000 minutes, 1,000 texts, and 30mb of data. A plan that at Verizon/AT&T would run you $89+ and that's without the data package. So I'm saving close to $60 a month with this plan."

—Laura, MoneySavingMom.com reader

"My husband and I successfully reduced our electric bill by $40 per month by doing two simple things. First, we installed compact fluorescent bulbs (CFLs) in all lamps and overhead light fixtures throughout the house. Second, we connected power strips to our televisions and computer equipment. We turn the power strips off when leaving the house for more than a few hours and also before retiring for the night. Other than the initial installation, these two energy savers require very little effort on our part, but produce $480 in annual savings!"

—Erin, MoneySavingMom.com reader

How to Stay Fit and Trim Without Breaking the Bank

- *Purchase Workout Equipment on Craigslist.* Never pay for brand-new workout equipment. Look in the newspaper or on Craigslist (or even at garage sales) for people who are getting rid of their used exercise equipment. We've saved hundreds of dollars by purchasing a weight gym and an elliptical through Craigslist—and they work just as good as new.

- *Find a Walking Buddy.* Walking costs nothing, but it's sometimes hard to stick with if you don't have the accountability. Ask a friend or neighbor to meet you regularly for fresh air and exercise—for free.

"We save $100 every two months by not having a gym membership. Instead, we get 'paid' to exercise. Each day when we go out for our four-mile walk, we take a couple of garbage sacks with us, and we pick up all the aluminum cans that we see on our walk. In one month, we've 'harvested' as much as $45 in recycled aluminum."

—Linda, MoneySavingMom.com reader

- *Use Exercise DVDs.* At only $5 to $15 each, exercise DVDs are much less expensive than a gym membership, and you can do them at home whenever you have time. Most libraries carry a good collection of workout DVDs, if you want to try them out before you buy. You can also find a number of free full-length workout videos online at exercisetv.tv.

- *Sign Up for SparkPeople.com.* If you're looking to lose weight or track your calorie intake, SparkPeople.com is a free online calorie tracker. You can set goals and track your progress, generate a menu based upon your specific calorie and dietary guidelines, or interact on the forums with others who are trying to lose weight.

"I love our local YMCA, but at $73/month for a family membership it's way out of our budget. I decided to apply for a job working in the child care department part time, so my personal membership is free. This amounts to a discount of $60/month, so we pay only $13/month for the rest of my family to be able to use the facilities. Not only does this save us $720/year, but it also adds a little extra income. My daughter loves to go and play with all her friends, and I get to be right there in the room with her while I work. It's really been a great experience for our whole family."

—Bekki, MoneySavingMom.com reader

CHAPTER NINE

EMBRACE TODAY

My husband was going through old financial statements recently and we were aghast to read the numbers. During the first year Jesse was in law school, there were six months when we made less than $900—and some months it was as low as $650. I recall that season of our lives fairly vividly, but seeing those numbers on paper again years later was a shock to our systems. Our rent alone during those months was over $500. I'm still not sure how we made it on so little! No wonder we rarely ate meat, used coupons at an incredible rate, went for months at a time without going out to eat or buying new clothes, and prayed a lot. Our commitment to live within our means and stay out of debt was hard, there's no doubt about it.

I remember we'd give 10 percent of our income to our local church, we'd pay our rent check and our basic utility bills, and then we'd pray that somehow the rest of the money would stretch until the next check would come. We had money set aside in the bank for law school, but we'd both committed that it was untouchable except for in the case of some life-or-death event. So we were determined to make do on whatever meager income we could scrounge up through part-time jobs.

During those years, we lived in a little basement apartment. I could plug the vacuum cleaner cord into one outlet and vacuum the entire apartment without ever switching to another. Our second vehicle broke down at the end of Jesse's first year of law school so for the next two years, we had only one vehicle. Jesse was gone at work and school all day and often late into the evenings. We knew hardly anyone in the town we lived in—in spite of many efforts to make friends— and there were not any safe places I could walk to from our apartment.

It would have been easy to become swallowed up by despair, and I won't pretend there weren't moments I felt sorry for myself or wished we could be living in better circumstances. However, I decided, with God's help, to try to make the most of what might seem like a less than ideal situation. And I learned to follow this rule:

RULE #7: CHOOSE CONTENTMENT

Maybe we didn't have money to go out, but I challenged myself to think up creative ways we could still have fun without spending money. We'd check out a movie from the library and have homemade pizza. In the winter, we'd brew some coffee, pop some popcorn, and play a board game. Sometimes, we'd go to the park with a picnic or we'd browse the book selection at Barnes and Noble.

We didn't have money to spend on decorating our home, but I still found ways to make it homey and inviting. I always tried to keep it clean and clutter-free. I figured even if it wasn't very pretty, at least it could smell nice and look clean! We tried to have music playing in the background, we burned candles, and I baked a lot. The smells and sounds made us feel richer, even if we didn't have a dollar to spare.

We couldn't afford fancy foods or restaurant meals, but that didn't mean we couldn't eat well. I had fun trying new recipes, searching out good deals, and stretching our grocery budget as far as possible. Instead of going out and buying things, I'd go to the library and check out a stack of books to read.

It was also in this little basement apartment that I first began blogging and tinkering around with online entrepreneurial things. Had it not been for the free time and lack of friends, I might never have considered pursuing blogging. And guess what? While holed up in that little basement apartment searching grocery deals online one day, I came upon this now-defunct savings forum raving about the deals at a store called CVS.

That discovery led to one thing and then another and, pretty soon, I had set up MoneySavingMom.com to teach others how to save money on their grocery bill, too. Little could I have dreamed that, in a few years, MoneySaving-Mom.com would grow to be one of the largest personal finance blogs on the web helping hundreds of thousands of families around the world lower their grocery bill and have a paradigm shift about money.

Yes, living in that little basement apartment in an unfamiliar town, barely squeaking by would never have been something I would have chosen for myself, but I'll always be grateful that God allowed me those three and a half years of learning to be content, learning to love simplicity, and learning to make the most of what I had.

A cheerful attitude can go a long way in less than ideal situations; you can either complain about the thorns or you can savor the roses that bloom in their midst.

HOW TO CULTIVATE CONTENTMENT

1. Choose to Count Your Blessings

We all have an innumerable list of things for which to be thankful. If you have clean drinking water, clothes to wear, food to eat, and a roof over your head, you have much more than many people have. It's so easy to focus on what we don't have, instead of being grateful for all we do have. And this just fosters a negative attitude.

2. Create a Gratitude List

When I am feeling discouraged and discontent, I challenge myself to think of things I can be thankful for. I'll usually pick a number—say ten—and start writing. At first, it's slow going, but once I get started, I have trouble stopping. Before I know it, my whole attitude will have changed because I begin to realize all sorts of wonderful things in my life I've been taking for granted.

3. Choose to Stop Comparing Yourself to Other People

There is always going to be someone who is skinnier, prettier, richer, more fit, more creative, more organized, and more energetic than you are. It's easy to spend your life wishing you were she. Wishing you had the hair she has, the body she has, the family she has, the house she has, the job she has, or whatever it is she has that you don't. But wishing you were she doesn't change that you are you.

4. Choose to be a Giver

When Jesse was in law school and our budget was so tight, we took a step of faith and committed to give 10 percent of our income to our local church. As Christians, we wanted to acknowledge that all we have and all we are is God's, so we gave the first 10 percent of our income to our local church and asked God to bless and multiply the remaining 90 percent.

Most of the time, we weren't sure how we were going to pay all of our bills, but every month, never fail, there was just enough to pay every necessary bill. We also found other ways to give on a very limited income—we bought extra groceries for free with coupons and gave them away to people who were struggling and we gave of our time to help those in need. It wasn't much, but it was what we could do, so we did it. And we found extreme joy and fulfillment in giving.

As our income has increased since those lean law school years, we've committed to continue to live simply and debt-free in order to give generously. The less we spend on ourselves, the more we have to give to others. Truly, living with outstretched hands freely giving has provided us far more rich satisfaction and fulfillment than we would ever find if we were to hoard things for ourselves.

Whether you make $10,000 a year or $250,000 a year, I encourage you to make giving one of your top priorities in your budget. Not only will you be blessed abundantly, but you might also find, as we have, that the more you give out, the more you have to give.

5. Choose to Bloom Where You're Planted

Contentment is a state of the heart, unaffected by outward circumstances. Contentment is a choice. You can choose to be miserable in your situation or you can choose to bloom where you are planted. You can choose to stop focusing on what you don't have and start being thankful for the many blessings you do have. As the saying goes, "Two men looked out of prison bars. One saw mud, the other saw stars."

It's all about perspective. Choose to bloom where you're planted—even if it seems like it's among thorns!

APPENDIX

10 TIPS FOR HAVING A SUCCESSFUL GARAGE SALE

1. Collect Clutter Year-Round

I mentioned in chapter 2 that we have an ongoing garage sale stash. When I come upon something we no longer need or use, and I don't know anyone to pass it on to, I stick it in a box in our garage. Once a box fills up, I start another. Without much effort at all, by the time it's the month of our annual garage sale, I usually have at least eight to ten boxes of stuff collected.

2. Have a Plan

A successful garage sale does not happen without organization. Two weeks before the sale, I go through my home from top to bottom and clear out clutter. Two to three days before the sale, I take an afternoon to price everything and organize it. And then the day before the sale, I devote a few hours to final organization, posting an ad on Craigslist, and getting the cash and signs together. Do not wait until the last minute to pull off a garage sale. Either it will flop or you'll run yourself ragged—or both.

3. Team Up

I always find friends or family to team up with when I do garage sales. Not only does this arrangement mean you have more stuff to sell and greater variety in sizes and items—it also means you have more help. Divvying up the responsibilities between three or four people makes a garage sale much more manageable. Plus, it just makes it more fun when you're doing it with friends and family!

4. Location, Location, Location!

If you don't live near a busy intersection, find a friend or relative who will let you host your sale at their home. There's no point in having a sale in an out-of-the-way location.

5. Timing Is Everything

Find out what days of the week are best for yard sales in your area. When we lived in Kansas City, I found people usually held sales on Friday and Saturday. However, where we live now, Thursdays are a big yard sale day and seem to garner the most traffic.

6. Mark Your Prices Clearly

It's easy to want to stick a big sign on a table saying that everything is a quarter, but in the long run it is much more efficient to put price stickers on everything. Instead of you having to make up prices on the spot, people will know exactly how much something is. In addition, some people are too shy to ask the price of an item, so you'll lose a sale if an item isn't marked.

7. Price Things to Sell

When I go to a garage sale, I expect to pay yard sale prices. Unless something is brand-new with the tags on, I am not going to pay more than a few quarters for it. When I am pricing my own items to sell, I always try to price things at what I feel would be a good bargain if I were buying the item at someone else's garage sale. I'd rather price something on the low end and have someone actually buy my item than to have twenty-five people pick up the item and put it back down on the table because it is too expensive.

8. Advertise Well

The marketing of your sale is usually the number-one factor in how well it does. You can have great items, great prices, and a great location, but if you don't tell people how to get there, they won't find it on their own. Make a number of quality, clearly readable signs with arrows that you put in conspicuous places to easily lead to your home. The brighter, bolder, and bigger the sign, the better.

Post a well-written ad on Craigslist the day before the sale and then repost a revised ad each day of the sale. Include specific items, brands, and sizes in your ad so that when people search for items on Craigslist, if they are looking for what you're selling—even if they aren't looking at garage sales—your item will pull up in searches for them.

9. Mark Things Down on the Last Day

Things are usually pretty picked over by the last day of the sale. That's the perfect opportunity to get creative and hand out rock-bottom bargains! We found that running "Fill a Bag for a Buck" or saying everything is half price is extremely effective.

10. Don't Forget the Cookies and Lemonade!

What better way to teach your children entrepreneurial skills and let them earn a little money in the process than to have them set up their own little cookie and lemonade stands at the sale? Or, if it's cold outside, try selling hot chocolate, coffee, and fresh cinnamon rolls. One yard sale, we even set up a pancake griddle and sold pancakes hot off the griddle on Saturday morning.

10 WAYS TO EARN AN EXTRA $100 PER MONTH

1. Paint Address Numbers on Curbs

Ever tried to find someone's house and had a hard time because you couldn't see any address numbers on the houses? Provide a solution to this problem by offering to paint house numbers on the curbs in front of houses. Get some paint and number stencils and write up a simple flier with details on your services. Canvas a few neighborhoods early in the week to let them know you'll be in their area on Saturday painting numbers on the curbs. You can charge $10 to $15 per house for this service and easily make $100 on a Saturday for just a few hours' worth of work. Be sure to check local laws as this may not be allowed in all municipalities.

2. Have a Booth at the Farmers' Market

Most towns and cities have a weekly farmers' market during the summer. Look into how much it would cost to set up a booth and sell baked goods or garden produce. I've seen people sell everything from jelly to quilts to tomatoes to plants.

3. Sell Your Clutter

Look around your house and see what items you are no longer using or could get rid of. Have a garage sale or sell these individual items on Craigslist or eBay. If you find that you enjoy selling your clutter for cash, you could turn this into a business! Kim says, "I let all of my friends know that I will sell their junk on eBay or Craigslist or Amazon.com for them. I keep 50 percent of the sale and they don't have to do the work of listing the item and mailing things to buyers. I have sold unopened bags of grout, DVDs, boxes of books, artwork, furniture, clothing, and lots of baby items. I even sold some medical equipment my husband no longer uses in his practice to a buyer in Mexico."

4. Become a Transcriptionist

Many professionals and companies working in health care, law, and business need transcriptionists. Universities also sometimes hire transcriptionists. If you have strong typing skills, this could be a great part-time job for you.

5. Walk Dogs or Board Pets

Advertise at pet stores or on Craigslist and see if there are pet owners in your area looking for someone to walk their dog on a regular basis or keep their pet for a few days while they are out of town. Call your local business bureau to confirm that a business of this type is allowed in your city.

6. Proctor Testing

Contact your local universities to see if they are in need of test proctors. If you have a college degree, you can usually qualify to proctor tests, and it's a very simple way to earn money.

7. Babysit

In most areas, you do not need a license to care for four or fewer children in your home. If you are a stay-at-home mom, caring for one child in addition to your own can bring in an extra $400 or more per month. If you don't have children of your own, being available to babysit during the day or in the evenings can provide many jobs. At least in our area, good babysitters with flexible schedules are in high demand.

8. Sell Plasma

If you are healthy and want to help others, you can earn at least $100 per month in most areas by selling plasma. Contact your local blood bank to find out more information on the requirements and pay.

9. Teach a Class

What are you skilled at? Teach that skill to others in a class setting and make a small profit off it. Many community centers and libraries allow you to have a room for free to teach classes. If you charge $5 or $10 per person, and ten people come each week, that's $200 to $400 in extra income each month.

10. Write

Some small magazines and newspapers have paid writing jobs available for those with decent writing and research skills. Local parents' magazines and newsletters are often looking for new content and do not require exclusive rights. While they often only pay $25 per article, if you submit the same article for publication in a hundred different parenting publications and ten of them publish it, that's $250 in profit from the one article. There are also many higher-paying freelance jobs available online or for larger publications, once you get your foot in the door.

Tip: If you're looking for freelancing work, check out ODesk.com and Elance.com for possible contract positions open in your area of expertise.

HELPFUL RESOURCES

It's been said, "You'll be the same person you were last year except for the books you read and the people you meet." Books have had a profound impact upon me. They've helped to shape the way I think and live. They stimulate me intellectually, they challenge me to improve as a person, and they teach me new concepts and ideas. I highly encourage you to set a goal to read at least one nonfiction book every month. If that seems impossible, then commit to reading just five minutes per day. I've found it works best for me to read early in the morning before I begin my day.

If you struggle to find time to read, listen to audio books. This is a great way to make the most of a commute or to keep your mind occupied while you're folding laundry or washing dishes.

RECOMMENDED READING

Goal Setting and Personal Responsibility

Flipping the Switch: Unleash the Power of Personal Accountability Using the QBQ!, John G. Miller, New York: G.P. Putnam's Sons, 2006

Today Matters: 12 Daily Practices to Guarantee Tomorrow's Success, John C. Maxwell, Paw Prints, 2008

Time and Life Management

Eat That Frog! 21 Great Ways to Stop Procrastinating and Get More Done in Less Time, Brian Tracy, Berrett-Koehler Publishers, 2007.

168 Hours: You Have More Time Than You Think, Laura Vanderkam, New York: Portfolio, 2010

Tell Your Time (ebook), Amy Lynn Andrews (available at http://amylynnandrews.com/tell-your-time/)

Simple Living

From Clutter to Clarity: Simplifying Life from the Inside Out, Nancy Twigg, Cincinnati, OH: Standard Pub, 2007

Organized Simplicity: The Clutter-Free Approach to Intentional Living, Tsh Oxenreider, Cincinnati, OH: Betterway Home, 2010

Finances

America's Cheapest Family Gets You Right on the Money: Your Guide to Living Better, Spending Less, and Cashing in on Your Dreams, Steve Economides and Annette Economides, New York: Three Rivers Press, 2007

Family Feasts for $75 a Week: A Penny-Wise Mom Shares Her Recipe for Cutting Hundreds from Your Monthly Food Bill, Mary Ostyn, Birmingham, AL: Oxmoor House, 2009

Miserly Moms: Living Well on Less in a Tough Economy, Jonni McCoy, Grand Rapids: Baker Pub. Group, 2009

Shift Your Habit: Easy Ways to Save Money, Simplify Your Life, and Save the Planet, Elizabeth Rogers and Colleen J. Howell, New York: Three Rivers Press, 2010

The Total Money Makeover: A Proven Plan for Financial Fitness, Dave Ramsey, Nashville, TN: Thomas Nelson Pub., 2009

RECOMMENDED WEBSITES

MoneySavingMom.com
SimpleMom.net
FlyLady.net
JonAcuff.com
DaveRamsey.com
GetRichSlowly.net

WORKSHEETS

Goal-Setting Worksheets

Time Budget Worksheets

Budgeting Worksheets

Price Book Worksheet

GOAL-SETTING WORKSHEET

STEP 1: BRAINSTORM FINANCIAL GOALS

STEP 2: CHOOSE 3 GOALS

1. This goal can be achieved in six to twelve months.

2. This goal can be achieved in a few years.

3. This goal is an audacious goal.

PERSONAL PRIORITIES LIST

THINGS I'M GIFTED AT AND/OR LOVE TO DO	THINGS I HOPE TO DO WITHIN FIVE TO TEN YEARS	THINGS THAT WILL BE IMPORTANT TO ME AT THE END OF MY LIFE

PERSONAL PRIORITIES LIST

THINGS I'M GIFTED AT AND/OR LOVE TO DO	THINGS I HOPE TO DO WITHIN FIVE TO TEN YEARS	THINGS THAT WILL BE IMPORTANT TO ME AT THE END OF MY LIFE

MY TOP PRIORITIES

1.
2.
3.
4.
5.
6.
7.
8.

TIME BUDGET WORKSHEET

Weekday Time Budget

	HOURS AVAILABLE	= 24 HOURS
SLEEP	-	=
MARGIN TIME	-	=
	-	=
	-	=
	-	=
	-	=
	-	=
	-	=
	-	=
	-	=0 HOURS

Weekend Time Budget

	HOURS AVAILABLE	= 24 HOURS
SLEEP	-	=
MARGIN TIME	-	=
	-	=
	-	=
	-	=
	-	=
	-	=
	-	=
	-	=
	-	=0 HOURS

WEEKLY TIME BUDGET WORKSHEET

	MONDAY	TUESDAY	WEDNESDAY	THURSDAY
MIDNIGHT				
1 AM				
2 AM				
3 AM				
4 AM				
5 AM				
6 AM				
7 AM				
8 AM				
9 AM				
10 AM				
11 AM				
NOON				
1 PM				
2 PM				
3 PM				
4 PM				
5 PM				
6 PM				
7 PM				
8 PM				
9 PM				
10 PM				
11 PM				

WEEKLY TIME BUDGET WORKSHEET

	FRIDAY	SATURDAY	SUNDAY
MIDNIGHT			
1 AM			
2 AM			
3 AM			
4 AM			
5 AM			
6 AM			
7 AM			
8 AM			
9 AM			
10 AM			
11 AM			
NOON			
1 PM			
2 PM			
3 PM			
4 PM			
5 PM			
6 PM			
7 PM			
8 PM			
9 PM			
10 PM			
11 PM			

BARE-BONES BUDGET WORKSHEET

BUDGET ITEM	MONTHLY*	WEEKLY*
FOOD		
Groceries		
Eating out		
BASIC UTILITIES		
Trash		
Water		
Electricity		
Gas		
Landline phone service		
Cell phone service		
SHELTER		
Mortgage/Rent		
Homeowner's/Renter's insurance		
TRANSPORTATION		
Car payment #1		
Car payment #2		
Public transportation		
Gas		
Auto repairs		
TOTALS		

*If you have an expense (such as groceries) that occurs weekly, you can convert it to a monthly expense by multiplying the weekly expense by 4.3. To convert a monthly expense to a weekly expense, divide the monthly expense by 4.3.

FULL-FLEDGED BUDGET WORKSHEET

BUDGET ITEM	MONTHLY*	WEEKLY*
CHARITABLE GIFTS		
Savings		
Emergency fund		
Retirement fund		
College fund		
House fund		
Car fund		
Baby fund		
HOUSING		
Mortgage/Rent		
Real estate taxes		
Homeowner's/Renter's insurance		
Repairs/Remodeling		
UTILITIES		
Electricity		
Water		
Gas		
Landline phone		
Cell phone		
Trash		
Cable		
Internet		
FOOD/ HOUSEHOLD ITEMS		
Groceries		
Eating out		
Household products		
Cosmetics		
TRANSPORTATION		
Car payment(s)		
Gas		
Repairs		
Car insurance		
License and taxes		
COLUMN TOTAL		

FULL-FLEDGED BUDGET WORKSHEET

BUDGET ITEM	MONTHLY*	WEEKLY*
HEALTH AND MEDICAL		
Disability insurance		
Health insurance		
Life insurance		
Doctor's visits		
Dental work		
Optometrist		
Contacts/Glasses		
Medications		
DEBT		
Credit card #1		
Credit card #2		
Credit card #3		
Line of credit		
Student loan 1		
Student loan 2		
Other		
PERSONAL/ RECREATION		
Clothing		
Child care/ Babysitting		
Hair care		
Education		
School Tuition/ Supplies		
Subscriptions		
Gifts		
Miscellaneous		
Vacation		
Entertainment		
Other		
COLUMN TOTAL		
GRAND TOTAL		

PRICE BOOK WORKSHEET

DATE	STORE	PRODUCT	SALE Y / N	PRICE $	SIZE / AMT	UNIT PRICE $ per

PRICE BOOK WORKSHEET

DATE	STORE	PRODUCT	SALE Y / N	PRICE $	SIZE / AMT	UNIT PRICE $ per

ACKNOWLEDGMENTS

I might be weird, but I always read the acknowledgments section in books I enjoy. It gives me a little peek into the life of the author. And, while I might be one of the only ones who reads the acknowledgments, I'm more than compelled to write one for this book. Because honestly, there would be no book if it weren't for these people:

Thank you to Anthony Ziccardi for believing in this book from the get-go—even long before *I* believed in it! To Sarah, the world's best agent, who caught the vision for this project, took me under her wing at the last minute, and helped me think like an author instead of a blogger. To Kathy, my wonderful editor, who worked tirelessly on this project and put up with many additional questions and requests from this novice author. To Catherine, who saw my initial rough draft, courageously told me "that's not good enough," and challenged me to aspire higher, change my mindset, and "own it."

My blog readers have taught me in leaps and bounds. The money-saving tips, frugal living ideas, and daily inspiration to live below one's means I glean from my readers have served, in large part, for much of the inspiration behind this book. Thank you, all of you, for taking time out of your busy lives to read my blog, interact in the comments, email in money-saving ideas, and give invaluable feedback on what I write (your constructive criticism has helped to shape me as a writer, thinker, and person). This book would have never happened were it not for you all. Thank you for making a long-time dream of mine a reality.

Where would I be without my team? I'm pretty certain I have some of the best and brightest minds in the universe who work for me—taking care of all the myriad of little behind-the-scenes details, brainstorming big-picture brilliance, and just generally helping me keep my head above water. Amy M., Amy A., Joy, Gretchen, Nathaniel, Megan, and Yvonne, I couldn't do what I do without you all.

A special thanks to my personal assistant, Megan. Thank you for listening to me bat around a hundred different ideas for this book, for shouldering a lot of extra work so I could focus on writing, and for creating a quiet, peaceful writing retreat in our basement for me where, in the early-morning hours, much of this manuscript was birthed.

Thank you also to some of the greatest friends the world has ever known: Jessica, it's been so fun to navigate the uncharted first-time author waters together with you. Susanna, we'd be sunk without you. Your willingness to come over every Tuesday and do whatever is needed at our house has ministered to us more than words can ever describe. Thank you for loving us—messes and all. Stacie, thank you for emailing me multiple times each week to check on me and make sure I was surviving.

I'm blessed to have been inspired and cheered on in this endeavor by women who've traveled the road of book writing before me. Sally, Angie, Shannon, Erin, Tsh, and Jennie, thanks for your sage advice and wise counsel.

I'm eternally indebted to my parents for requiring us to work hard and be assets to our family from an early age. Thank you, Mom and Dad, for not giving us everything we wanted, but teaching us instead the value of money and work. Your commitment to living debt-free and giving generously has forever influenced me. And I'm blessed with wonderful extended family and in-laws, too! As babies and spouses keep being added, the names and numbers grow, so a list is likely soon to be outdated, but thank you, each of you, for everything you mean to me.

My children, Kathrynne, Kaitlynn, and Silas, are the most adorable and precious children on the planet. (A mother is allowed license for bias!) They light up my life, keep me grounded, force me to my knees, and remind me that life is short. I love the opportunity I get as a work-at-home, home-schooling mom, to stay home with them all day, every day.

Jesse, you're my solid rock, my sounding board, and my best friend. Thank you for being so excited about this project from the get-go and for all the sacrifices you've made to see it to completion. You've walked out the principles this book espouses day in and day out with me—even when it was hard, monotonous, and grueling. Without you by my side, there would be no book. It sounds trite, but it's absolutely true: I don't deserve such a wonderful husband. Yes, we may have our disagreements and "hearty discussions" on occasion, but we are completely incomplete without each other.

Finally, I owe all I have and all I am to my Creator. Without Him, I am nothing. I want to faithfully steward what He has given me so that someday I may hear the words, "Well done."

All of the author's proceeds from this book will be donated to Compassion International, an organization that exists as a Christian child advocacy ministry releasing children from spiritual, economic, social, and physical poverty and enabling them to become responsible, fulfilled adults. Founded by Rev. Everett Swanson in 1952, Compassion began providing Korean War orphans with food, shelter, education, and health care, as well as Christian training. Today, Compassion International helps more than one million children in twenty-six countries. For more information, visit Compassion.com.